KEYBOARD
INSTRUMENTS
Studies in Keyboard Organology
1500–1800

KEYBOARD INSTRUMENTS

Studies in Keyboard Organology
1500–1800

EDITED BY
EDWIN M. RIPIN

DOVER PUBLICATIONS, INC.
NEW YORK

Published in Canada by General Publishing Company, Ltd., 30 Lesmill Road, Don Mills, Toronto, Ontario.
Published in the United Kingdom by Constable and Company, Ltd., 10 Orange Street, London WC2H 7EG.

This Dover edition, first published in 1977, is an unabridged republication of the work originally published by the Edinburgh University Press in 1971 under the title *Keyboard Instruments: Studies in Keyboard Organology*. A new Preface has been written for the present edition, and several additions have been made to Edmund A. Bowles' article.

International Standard Book Number: 0-486-23363-4
Library of Congress Catalog Card Number: 76-29605

Manufactured in the United States of America
Dover Publications, Inc.
180 Varick Street
New York, N.Y. 10014

Preface to the First Edition

This collection of essays was assembled with three principal ends in view. The first and most obvious desire was to publish in a single volume a group of specialized articles dealing with much-debated topics in the history of keyboard instruments. Secondly, there existed a number of unique surviving instruments of which no adequate descriptions had ever been published and for which no such descriptions would be likely to see print if they were not directly solicited for a specialized collection. Finally, it seemed desirable to attempt to provide a survey of the present state of keyboard organology.

To be sure, the more traditional organological methods —including the examination of contemporary writings, archival documents, iconographic materials, and the music written to be played on the instruments under consideration —are employed in working with keyboards. However, the current technique seems to be distinguished from that of earlier times and that in most other areas of organology by the constant recourse to the surviving instruments as the primary documents and by the continual checking against the instruments themselves of the conclusions drawn from other sources. Furthermore, there is in keyboard organology a distinct trend toward the assimilation of the largest possible bodies of data —a casting of the widest possible net —so that even the examination of a single instrument occurs within the context of numerous similar or analogous examples and all the surviving written and pictorial evidence. The findings that result from taking this approach are necessarily technical in nature and frequently seem to partake more of the tone normally associated with the physical sciences than they do of that customary in the humanities. Although this may, perhaps, be deplored—in that it appears to be part of a trend toward the dehumanization of all fields of scholarly effort—it seems, on the contrary, to provide belated confirmation of the Ancients' correctness in placing music together with sciences of number, geometry, and astronomy, in the Quadrivium.

The approach to the subject embodied in the present methods of keyboard organology is not, of course, new. It is apparent at every turn in the pioneering writings of A. J. Hipkins, who is surely the patron saint of all subsequent toilers in this rich vineyard. However, it was not until after the Second World War that the splendid example of Hipkins' *History of the Pianoforte* (1896) was accorded any widespread emulation, notably in numerous fine articles in the *Galpin Society Journal* (vol. 1, 1948), and in the three books that form the canon of contemporary keyboard studies : Donald Boalch's *Makers of the Harpsichord and Clavichord* (1956), Raymond Russell's *The Harpsichord and Clavichord* (1959), and Frank Hubbard's *Three Centuries of Harpsichord Making* (1965).

It is especially fitting that a collection of articles of this kind and on this subject should appear under the auspices of Edinburgh University, to whom Raymond Russell bequeathed his uniquely representative collection of harpsichords and clavichords, and where these instruments are now so splendidly housed and exhibited.

It remains only to thank the contributors for their articles and for their extraordinary patience in bearing with editorial coercion. Especial gratitude is owed to Peter Williams, who, in addition to contributing an article, has acted as my liaison with the Press and vastly lightened the burdens of seeing this collection into print.

EDWIN M. RIPIN
New York, 1971

Note on Measurements
Numerals in parentheses give inch equivalents of the preceding measurements in millimetres.

Preface to the Dover Edition

The Dover edition of *Keyboard Instruments: Studies in Keyboard Organology*, *1500–1800* differs from the 1971 edition principally in the addition of six representations of keyboard instruments discovered since the original printing of *A Checklist of Fifteenth-century Representations of Stringed Keyboard Instruments* by Edmund A. Bowles. Other changes include the addition of dates to the subtitle and the placement of the plates for each article immediately following the text rather than as a group at the end of the volume, and the consequent alteration of pagination. Citation to this edition should specify that page numbers refer to the reprinted edition.

The death of the editor of this volume in November, 1975, has deprived the reprinted edition of his guidance through the press.

ARLEY L. RIPIN
New York, 1976

Contents

The Specious Uniformity of Italian Harpsichords

JOHN BARNES
*Curator, The Russell Collection of Harpsichords and
Clavichords, Edinburgh*

Every commentator on the Italian school of harpsichord-building
has remarked on the comparatively small amount of development
that took place in Italian instruments between the sixteenth and eighteenth centuries. The reason that most of the surviving sixteenth-
century harpsichords are Italian is, indeed, that they sufficiently
resembled the later ones to be retained in musical use until the beginning of the nineteenth century. It should not, however, be
assumed that there were no significant changes during the three
centuries covered by surviving examples or that the earlier harpsichords have reached us intact. Close examination reveals a surprising number of alterations which have to be considered when trying
to reconstruct the dispositions, compasses, and scalings that these
instruments originally possessed.

The Raymond Russell Collection of the University of Edinburgh
contains two Italian harpsichords, one inscribed 'Stephanus Bol-
cionius Pratensis 1627', the other anonymous but probably also
from the first half of the seventeenth century.[1] The alterations to
be observed in the first, which was fraudulently equipped with three
keyboards, are of a different kind from those which form the subject of this article, but one original feature is of interest because of
the light it throws on the original state of the anonymous instrument. The Bolcioni originally had only a single keyboard and two
unison stops, but the original box slides which guide the jacks
were not discarded when the instrument was altered.[2] The spacing
of the jacks in an Italian harpsichord is usually such that 12 jacks
occupy an octave-span of about 165 mm (6.5), but the spacing of
the slots in the Bolcioni slides yields a reduced 'octave' which
varies from 159 mm (6.25) in the bass to 155 mm (6.12) in the
treble. Originally, there were 53 jacks in each row rather than the
52 required for the present C/E–g′′′ compass. The explanation is
doubtless that, like so many other harpsichords and virginals of the
early seventeenth century, the Bolcioni was fitted with divided
accidentals for the purpose of extending the range of modulations
possible with the meantone system of tuning. The middle octaves
of such instruments have 13, 14, or 15 notes, depending on the
number of accidentals divided. The most likely compass using 53
notes is C/E–c′′′ with a broken octave (additional F♯ and G♯
behind the notes playing D and E) in the bass and six divided

accidentals in the upper octaves : d#/e♭, g#/a♭, a#/b♭, d#′/e♭′, g#′/a♭′, and a#′/b♭′.

The anonymous harpsichord invites suspicion because it has a chromatic compass C–d‴. The alterations are not very obvious, and the keyboard could easily be believed to be original;[3] but a close inspection reveals that the balance mortises of the keys are not as worn as one would expect from the hollowing of the ivories. Also, the six highest accidentals have tops made in two pieces, neatly glued together and mounted on one lever. The string plan has been altered, the evidence being a series of plugged holes in the treble half of the soundboard bridge (matched by similar alterations of the hitchpin positions) and the fact that the middle strings are not quite parallel to the others. Since there are no corresponding plugged holes in the wrestplank bridge, it must be a replacement.

The plugged holes in the soundboard bridge are more closely spaced than the present strings. When the original string spacing is reconstructed from the unaltered pins in the bass and the plugged holes in the treble, it is found to be uniform, with 12 notes occupying only 147 mm (5.8). As with the Bolcioni, this can only mean that the original keyboard had divided accidentals. A total of 57 string pairs is indicated by the plugged holes, but there may have been 58 if the bridge had originally been a little longer in the treble. The most likely compass for 58 notes would be C/E–f‴ with a broken octave and six divided accidentals, probably the same ones as postulated for the Bolcioni.

Such a keyboard would have been obsolete in the later years of the eighteenth century, when the short octave was abandoned and well-tempered tunings had replaced meantone. A clever harpsichord-maker, however, could have brought the instrument up to date for much less than the cost of a new one. In actual fact, the modernising of this harpsichord involved making a new keyboard, although the ivory and ebony facings of the original keys were utilised, resulting in the composite sharp tops, which were bunched at the extreme treble where they would be less noticeable. Parts of the old keyframe were probably re-used as well. The original closely pinned wrestplank bridge and the closely spaced jack guides (probably box slides) were replaced. The new, normally spaced jack guides took the form of separate upper and lower guides of Italian pattern, which in itself is probably an indication of eighteenth-century work. The old tuning-pin holes are presumably to be found plugged underneath a capping piece which now covers part of the wrestplank. The original jacks probably survived the eighteenth-century alteration, but this cannot now be verified since unfortunately, they did not survive a 1948 restoration.

Although the spacing between the jacks was increased, the narrow spacing of the soundboard bridge pins in the bass and tenor was retained. This resulted in a misalignment of the strings in the middle of the compass, which was corrected by repinning part of the treble. The new keyboard had the same overall width as the old, but the change of compass had the additional effect of reducing the scale of the longer c″ string from 282 mm (11.1) to 264 mm (10.4), so that it conformed nicely to eighteenth-century practice. After these alterations, the octave doubling of the string lengths was still almost as accurate as that on a specially made instrument.

Another harpsichord which exhibits interesting alterations is the Antonius Baffo of 1574 in the Victoria and Albert Museum, London.[4] Its keyboard compass was originally C/E–f‴, which was subsequently altered to GG/BB–c‴ by the following procedure:

1. Key C/E and keys c‴ to e‴ inclusive were stripped of their keyplates and arcades, and the bare levers were discarded. A board 376 mm × 93 mm × 14 mm (14.8 × 3.65 × 0.55) was prepared from which to cut the new keys GG/BB–E required for extending the bass. (This board was beech, whereas the original keys were sycamore.)

2. The keyframe was cut at the line between c‴ and d‴. This left the three rails unsupported, but the tie running from front to back which had just been removed was refitted, even though it was 8 mm (0.3) too short to fit perfectly. A simple extension to the frame was constructed at the bass end, utilising the portion of balance rail removed from the treble end.

3. The new uncut keys of the bass section were marked out, drilled in position, and then cut apart, after which the old arcades and keyplates were fitted. Key f‴ was lengthened slightly to form the new full-width c‴, and the balance pin was repositioned to suit it.[5]

This harpsichord underwent another alteration, possibly at the same time. There are clear marks on the soundboard showing that the instrument at one time possessed an octave register, and there is convincing evidence that this was its original state. The positions of the octave hitchpins are very obvious; above the middle of the compass it is also possible to see where the octave bridge pins were, since the holes drilled for them penetrated the soundboard. If the octave bridge had been higher in the bass than in the treble, this would explain why the holes, drilled carefully to constant depth by using a stop, would not show in the bass.[6] The position of the octave bridge on the wrestplank is similarly revealed by pinholes, permitting an accurate measurement of the octave scaling. Assuming that the octave jacks plucked toward the right, the scale was 396 mm (15.6), which agrees with that of the unison strings, assuming that these were plucked to the left.

The layout of this harpsichord is an almost exact antithesis of Flemish practice. The wrestplank bridges were close together, with both sets of tuning pins in front of the unison wrestplank bridge.[7] With this arrangement, it does not make sense to pluck the shorter set of strings with the farther row of jacks, so it must be assumed that the octave jacks formed the front row. One of the box slides has the word 'Otava' written on it, and this slide was certainly in the front position when it and the wrest-plank were being bored by woodworms.

When the second unison choir was substituted for the octave, the octave bridges and hitchpins were removed, and the jacks of the front row were lengthened so that their plectra would reach the level of the unison bridges. The substitution of a second unison for the original octave register and the keyboard alteration (which had the effect of raising the pitch by a fourth, if it is assumed that the strings themselves remained tuned to the same pitches) were both modernisations, in that they made the instrument similar to those being built at the time the rebuilding was done.[8]

A very similar history can be deduced for the 1531 harpsichord by Alessandro Trasuntino in the Donaldson Collection of the Royal College of Music, London. Like the 1574 Baffo, the Trasuntino has the plugged hitchpin holes of an octave register in its soundboard. The line of these holes and that of the bridge, whose position can now only be inferred, fit neatly with the positions of the three fine roses. Since only 44 hitchpin holes can be found, the octave stop presumably reached only to b''. Confirmation that there was only one unison choir of strings, and that it was in the left-hand position, is found in a short extension piece to the soundboard bridge, which has been added to carry the topmost string. (This eliminates the possibility that the octave register reverted to unison pitch for the six top notes.) The wrestplank bridge is obviously a replacement, since it has no corresponding extension, differs in its moulding, and has no holes or slots through which the octave strings could pass.

A thoroughgoing keyboard alteration has also taken place in which the original keys and balance rail were completely replaced. The part of the keybed which appears to be original consists of the front and back rails, the slotted rear guide rack, and the endpieces. Strips of wood have been glued under all these parts to raise the keyboard by 10 mm (0.4), probably for the purpose of bringing the octave jacks to the level of the unison strings without having to lengthen them individually. The balance rail, however, must date from the time when these strips were added, since their absence would leave it protruding below the level of the original parts of the keyframe. The added strips raise the balance rail about 3 mm

(0.1) clear of the baseboard of the harpsichord. The key levers are made of the same wood as the balance rail and clearly date from the same period, although the keyplates and arcades are probably original.[9]

The original compass of the 1574 Baffo harpsichord was established by the presence of most of the keys and balance rail. In the Trasuntino they are missing, and no such positive deduction may be made. We can surely assume, however, that the original compass was different from the present G G / B B–c‴, and it is highly probable that it was the same as that of the Baffo, C / E–f‴. If this is so, and if the present unison wrestplank bridge is in the same position as that of the original, then Trasuntino must have used a scale of 363 mm (14.3).

Another harpsichord by Alessandro Trasuntino is in the Collection of the Brussels Conservatoire. This instrument appears to have had an even more complicated history of alterations, the elucidation of which would be difficult without reference to the Donaldson instrument just described. The Brussels Trasuntino was made in 1538 and is strung at present with one unison and one octave choir, although at one time it had two unison registers, as shown by the still-extant bridge pins and hitchpins for a second unison register. It is easy to see from their inferior workmanship that both of the wrestplank bridges and the octave soundboard bridge are replacements. The unison soundboard bridge, however, is finely made and the hitchpin holes in the soundboard for the octave stop also have the accurate placement that one expects to find in original work.

The original specification is suggested by examination of the unison soundboard bridge. Conveniently, a consistent difference can be observed between the placing of the two sets of pins, one set being farther away from the ridge of the moulding than the other, presumably original, set. The conclusion that only one set is original is confirmed by consistent differences in the sets of unison hitchpins. Since the octave hitchpin holes in the soundboard are very accurately placed along a scribed line and have every appearance of originality, we may safely conclude that the harpsichord was built with one unison and one octave register.

This specification has clearly been changed at some later date to give two unisons, and the original octave bridges and hitchpins were probably removed at this time. The original unison wrestplank bridge seems to have been replaced at the same time because the present bridge has had pins for two choirs of strings. The reason that the original bridge was not retained may possibly have been that the holes through which the octave strings passed were in the way of the new set of pins. Instead of lengthening the octave jacks individually when converting them to play the new unison strings at a higher level, battens 5 mm (0.2) thick were placed under the keyboard, and the old unison jacks shortened instead.

Later still, the octave choir was reinstated with new octave bridges on the wrestplank and the soundboard and with new hitch-pins, mostly in the original holes, yielding the state in which it is now found. The unison wrestplank bridge was drilled to allow the octave strings to pass through it, and the second set of bridge pins had to be withdrawn in order to drill these holes.

There is one feature which suggests that the work was performed by someone unfamiliar with the Italian practice of placing the octave jacks in the front row : the reinstated octave register uses the back row of jacks, marked with a double line, which were shortened for this purpose.

The present keyboard is dated 1669 and has a compass of D–e''', without e♭''' (50 notes). This is an unusual compass, inexplicable in terms of the demands of written music, but it may have been chosen simply to give a desired pitch. The scale then became 284 mm (11.2). The most likely original compass is C/E–f''', which would give a scale of 318 mm (12.5) with the present position of the unison wrestplank bridge.

The same combination of C/E–f''' compass, long scale, and a disposition of one unison and one octave has been established for the 1585 harpsichord by Alexander Bortolotti in the collection of the Brussels Conservatoire, which still has its octave bridges.[10] Thomas and Rhodes[11] give the string lengths for its present compass of GG/BB–c''' but acknowledge in their postscript that the original compass was C/E–f'''. When this is taken into account, the scale becomes 351 mm (13.8). Thomas and Rhodes found evidence that the right-hand unison was not original, a finding corroborated by the fact that the octave scale matched that of the left-hand unison.

The effect of the alterations to these four sixteenth-century harpsichords was to give them the disposition and scale appropriate to the seventeenth and eighteenth centuries (although the Baffo scale still remained rather long by eighteenth-century standards). Doubtless the instruments owe their survival to these successful modifications, which would have given them a new lease of life. It is, of course, their altered states that are recorded in the current textbooks, giving rise to the erroneous belief that sixteenth-century Italian makers used shorter scales for their harpsichords than for their virginals. Most sixteenth-century virginal scales lie between 307 mm (12.1)[12] and 390 mm (15.4),[13] and some of the apparent exceptions may be of later date.[14] The scales deduced above for the four harpsichords cover a similar range.

An inescapable question raised by the long scales deduced for these four sixteenth-century harpsichords is that of their intended pitch. It is particularly noticeable that the practice of doubling the string length for each octave is accurately observed in both unison and octave registers of Italian harpsichords except for the lowest five or six notes, which are foreshortened as a matter of convenience. That makers observed this rule, usually with a deviation of less than ± 2 per cent, is an indication that it had some practical importance. Undoubtedly, their intention was to obtain the best tone from their strings by stressing them near to the breaking point in all parts of the compass. Thomas and Rhodes have explained in physical terms why this improves the tuning accuracy of the harmonics.[15] Naturally, the maker has to use a safety factor so that his strings will have a reasonable working life. If for any particular instrument we can decide what material was used for the strings, we can come very close to determining the pitch that the maker had in mind when he set out to conform rigidly to a particular scale.

Italian harpsichords of the eighteenth century have scales of about 266 mm (10.5) for the longer choir of strings, and we have evidence for the belief that the pitches then in use were near to our modern standard. This scale and pitch are consistent with the use of copper-alloy strings at a tension two or three semitones below that at which a typical copper-alloy string can be expected to break. (The safety margin needs to be at least two semitones because an increase of humidity will often cause an instrument's pitch to rise by a semitone.) There is, therefore, good cause to believe that copper alloys were the choice of the eighteenth-century Italian makers.[16] The general design of Italian instruments is so consistent that it is difficult to believe that the material of the wire differed in the eighteenth century from that used in the sixteenth and seventeenth centuries. The long scales must then be accepted as evidence of pitch levels considerably lower than anything which might be regarded as 8' pitch. The scale of the Brussels Trasuntino, on these assumptions, implies a pitch approximately three semitones below $a' = 440$ cps; those of the Donaldson Trasuntino and the Brussels Bortolotti imply pitches approximately five semitones below modern pitch; and Baffo's scale of 1574 suggests a pitch approximately seven semitones below modern pitch.[17]

An explanation may here be offered of the fact that many long-scale virginals have escaped the alterations found in long-scale harpsichords. A satisfactory method of raising the pitch of the virginals was to fit iron wire in the upper part of the compass in the Flemish manner. The bass presented no problems because the strings of a virginal are restricted in length in order to produce an instrument of convenient size, and the bass strings do, in fact, sound better at the higher pitch. Since a virginal has fewer strings than a harpsichord, the extra tension would not be a serious problem, provided that thin wire was used.[18] Nevertheless, some virginals are found to have compass alterations or moved bridges, suggesting that this simple expedient was either not universally known or not universally approved.

The earliest surviving signed and dated harpsichord and, consequently, one of the best known of all sixteenth-century Italian instruments, is the Hieronymus Bononiensis of 1521 in the Victoria and Albert Museum.[19] This instrument now has an unusual keyboard range of C/E–d''' (47 notes) and the two unison registers which one tends to expect on Italian instruments. Its original state must in part remain conjectural since the present keyboard, jacks, slides, and wrestplank are all replacements.[20] However, in the light of the alterations to harpsichords by Trasuntino, Baffo, and Bortolotti, we need not be too surprised to find that here also the present disposition represents a later modification. About 10 mm (0.4) has been removed from the rail that supports the front edge of the soundboard and a similar amount gained by fitting a narrower wrestplank. (A shallow rabbet in the case appears to indicate the position of the original wrestplank.) This is the usual method for gaining room for an extra register, and we may therefore be fairly confident that there was originally only one unison stop.[21]

The instrument is too small to have had a C/E–f''' compass, so the original was almost certainly either the familiar C/E–c''' (45 notes) or the once-common F–f''', lacking low F♯ and G♯ (47 notes).[22] Unfortunately, the present condition of the instrument is consistent with either possibility. The cypress veneer on the wrestplank was probably transferred from the original, but it is not clear which of the two rows of tuning pins was original and both now have 47 pins (with two extra plugged holes at the left end of the front row). Between the cheeks, the keyboard space measures 726 mm (28.6), which implies keyblocks about 38 mm (1.5) wide for the C/E–c''' compass or about 20 mm (0.8) wide for the F–f''' compass, both of which widths are reasonable. Any estimate of the relative probability of the two compasses must therefore be made on evidence derived from other instruments.

Although the four sixteenth-century harpsichords examined in this article do not, perhaps, by themselves form a completely reliable basis for conjecture, they do agree in suggesting a prevalence of low pitches, and the conclusion is inescapable that we have been seeing the sixteenth-century instruments not as they were originally built but as they were altered to conform to harpsi-chord-building practices of the seventeenth and eighteenth cen-turies. When it is recognized that similar alterations are likely to have been made to the Hieronymus Bononiensis, the most likely original compass would seem to be F–f''', lacking low F♯ and G♯, which would imply a scale of 340–360 mm (13.5–14) and a pitch about five semitones below that used today.

Acknowledgements

I am indebted to Professor Sidney Newman, Emeritus Professor of Music, University of Edinburgh, to Peter Thornton, Keeper of the Department of Furniture and Woodwork of the Victoria and Albert Museum, to Monsieur René de Maeyer, Curator of the Brussels Conservatoire Collection, and to Mrs Elizabeth Wells, Curator of the Donaldson Collection of the Royal College of Music, London, for permission to publish the results of my examinations of instruments in their care.

NOTES AND REFERENCES

1 The Bolcioni is illustrated in P. James *Early Keyboard Instruments From Their Beginnings to the Year 1820* (London 1930) plate XLV. Both instruments are illustrated and described in *The Russell Collection and Other Early Keyboard Instruments in Saint Cecilia's Hall, Edinburgh* (Edinburgh 1968) nos. 4, 2.

2 The forger needed three slides and solved his problem by slicing one of the pair horizontally along its length.

3 Strictly speaking, one can never be sure that a part is original with-out the testimony of the maker. In practice, parts are assumed to be original when they conform to what is known of traditional practice and when there is no evidence of non-originality.

4 Illustrated in Russell *The Harpsichord and Clavichord* (London 1959) plate 7, and in P. James, op. cit., plate XXXV.

5 The remarkable condition of this harpsichord may be judged from the fact that the cloth strip under the front of the keys still comes to an end beneath key E, and a different kind of cloth is found under the keys GG/BB–E♭. The large strip therefore predates the alteration of the compass, and there is a strong probability that it is original and has remained undisturbed for almost 400 years.

6 The unison bridge is tapered, being 17 mm (0.67) high in the bass and only 13 mm (0.53) high in the treble.

7 A similar arrangement is preserved in the 1585 Bortolotti harpsi-chord discussed below. It may be seen in Mersenne *Harmonie universelle* (Paris 1636) 'Liure Troisiesme, des Instrumens à Chordes,' p. 111, reproduced in F. Hubbard *Three Centuries of Harpsichord Making* (Cambridge, Mass., 1965) plate X. Both original wrestplank bridges of the Baffo have disappeared, but presumably the octave strings passed through holes in the unison wrestplank bridge, as they do in the 1585 Bortolotti. The present wrestplank bridge is a rather crude replacement and does not follow the line of the original.

8   Further alterations of a still later period, when some 250 mm (10) was roughly cut from the tail and the compass crudely enlarged to C–f′′′, do not concern us here.

9   The altered keyboard was fitted with pedal pulldowns to notes C, D, E, F, G, A, B♭ and B.

10   Illustrated in Russell, op. cit., plate 8.

11   W. R. Thomas and J. J. K. Rhodes 'The string scales of Italian keyboard instruments' *Galpin Society Journal* xx (1967) 48.

12   Siculus, 1540, Benton Fletcher Collection, London.

13   Antegnato, 1537, Victoria and Albert Museum, London.

14   A virginal with a scale of 276 mm (10.9) at Ingatestone Hall, Essex, is plausibly attributed to Bonafinis—see F. G. Emmison 'A virginal by (?) Franciscus Bonafinis, 1560, at Ingatestone Hall' *Galpin Society Journal* xvii (1964) 109—but the ink inscription on the bottom giving the date 1560 is questionable.

15   Op. cit., p. 58.

16   Supporting this contention, the anonymous inventor of the Cembalo Angelico (see Russell, op. cit., p. 131, for a translation of the booklet published in Rome in 1775) refers to 'the sliding of the velvet-like plectrum on the brass string' (Article 6, section 11), as though the material of the wire should be taken for granted. Also, M. Corrette *Le Maitre de clavecin* (Paris 1753) p. 82, says that when c′′′ is 'only 5 inches long, it is necessary to string the harpsichord with yellow [brass] strings...' See Hubbard, op. cit., p. 90.

17   It is interesting to notice a low pitch associated with an octave stop, giving way to a higher pitch with only unisons. The change in general brilliance would probably not have been very great.

18   It has been suggested (Thomas and Rhodes, op. cit., p. 52) that the iron stringing of long-scale virginals was the makers' intention and that these virginals were originally built to sound at 8′ pitch. The existence of long-scaled harpsichords raises serious doubts about the validity of this theory.

19   R. Russell *Victoria and Albert Museum, Catalogue of Musical Instruments* 1, *Keyboard Instruments* (London 1968) no. 1.

20   The present top key is made from two keys glued together, and part of the number 50 is visible on the right-hand half. An inspection of the keyframe confirms that the keyboard has been cut down from one with the common 50-note compass C/E–f′′′ taken from another instrument. The jack slides, each of which now has three slots covered, may well have come from the same source. The jacks appear to have come from several instruments.

21   The single-register Italian harpsichord is the subject of Mr Hellwig's article elsewhere in this volume.

22   The balance rail of the 1537 Antegnati virginal in the Victoria and Albert Museum (Russell *Victoria and Albert Museum Catalogue*, no. 2) shows this to have been its original compass. The F–f′′′ compass also appears in the intarsia of a clavichord executed between 1479 and 1482 on the wall of the Studiolo of Federigo da Montefeltro in the Ducal Palace at Urbino. See below, plate 12 of Dr Bowles' article elsewhere in this volume.

A Checklist of Fifteenth-century Representations of Stringed Keyboard Instruments

EDMUND A. BOWLES

I.B.M. Corporation, Bethesda, Maryland

CLAVICHORD

1. Berlin, Bodemuseum.
   Carved Angel in the altarpiece from the Cathedral at Minden.
   Date. 1425.
   Documentation. Herbert Heyde 'Die Musikinstrumentendarstellung auf dem Mindener Altar' *Beiträge für Musikwissenschaft* VI (1964) 32–33.

2. Naples, San Giovanni a Carbonara, Caraccioli Chapel.
   Leonardo da Besozzo and Perrineto da Benevento *Lives of the Hermit Saints* (fresco).
   Date. Soon after 1433.
   Documentation. L. Serra 'Gli affreschi della rotonda di San Giovanni a Carbonara' *Bolletino d'Arte* IV (1909–10) 121 ff.; P. Toesca *La pittura e la miniatura nella Lombardia* (Milan 1912) pp. 474 f.; R. van Marle *The Development of the Italian Schools of Painting* VII (The Hague 1926) p. 148; E. M. Ripin 'The early clavichord' *The Musical Quarterly* LIII (1967) 520.

3. Shrewsbury, Saint Mary's Church.
   Carved Angel (wooden corbel at nave ceiling).
   Date. c. 1440.
   Documentation. D. H. S. Cranage *An Architectural Account of the Churches of Shropshire* II² (Shropshire 1908) p. 925; F. W. Galpin *Old English Instruments of Music*, 4th rev. ed. by T. Dart (London 1965) p. 91; H. Panum *Stringed Instruments of the Middle Ages*, tr. J. Pulver (London, n.d.) p. 322.

4. Paris, Bibliothèque Nationale, MS lat. 7295, fol. 129r.
   Henri Arnaut de Zwolle *Compositio clavicordii.*
   Date. 1436–54.
   Documentation. G. le Cerf 'Note sur le clavicorde et le dulce melos' *Revue de Musicologie* XV (1931) 1–9, 99–105; G. le Cerf and E. R. Labande *Instruments de musique au xvᵉ siècle : les traités d'Henri-Arnaut de Zwolle et de diverses anonymes* (Paris 1932) pp. vii–xvii; Ripin, op. cit., 520.

5. Warwick, Saint Mary's Church.
   John Prudd, Musician-Angels (stained-glass window).

The representations are reproduced on plates numbered to correspond with their numbers in this list.

Date. 1439–47.

Documentation. W. Bentley 'Notes on the musical instruments figured in the windows of the Beauchamp Chapel' *Transactions and Proceedings of the Birmingham Archaeological Society* LIII (1928) 167–72; C. F. Hardy 'On the music in the painted glass of the windows of the Beauchamp Chapel at Warwick' *Archaeologica* LXI² (1909) 583–614.

6. Coburg, Gymnasium Casimirianum, MS Cas. 43, fol. 3r.
   Heinrich Czun, Copy of manuscript by Otto von Passau, *The Twenty-Four Elders.*

   Date. 1448.

   Documentation. F. G. Kaltwasser *Die Handschriften der Bibliothek des Gymnasium Casimirianum und der Scheres-Zieritz-Bibliothek* (Coburg 1960) pp. 105 ff.; W. Schmidt *Die vierundzwanzig Alten Ottos von Passau* (Leipzig 1938); G. Schünemann 'Die Musikinstrumente der 24 Alten' *Archiv für Musikforschung* I (1936) 56.

7. Stuttgart, Württemburgische Landesbibliothek, MS phil. et poet. Q52, fol. 65v.
   Hugo von Reutlingen, *Flores musice.*

   Date. after 1467.

   Documentation. J. Handschin 'Das Pedalklavier' *Zeitschrift für Musikwissenschaft* XVII (1935) esp. 419; K. Löffler *Die Handschriften des Klosters Zwiefalten* (Linz 1931) p. 88.

8. Uppland, Tierp Church.
   Musician-Angel (fresco).

   Date. c. 1470.

   Documentation. T. Norlind *Bildur ur svenska musikens historia från äldsta tid till medeltidens slut* (Stockholm 1947) p. 245; H. Cornell and S. Wallin *Målningar av Tierpgruppen* (Stockholm 1966) p. 100; Per-Anders Hellquist *Musik-motiv i Sveriges Kyrkokonst före år 1600, Ett försök till inventering* (unpublished).

9. Lovran, Saint George's Church.
   Musician-Angel (fresco on presbytery vault).

   Date. 1470–79.

   Documentation. B. Fučić *Istarske freske* (Zagreb 1963) esp. p. 22 and fig. 21; K. Kos 'Muzicirajoči Angeli v Cerkvi sv. Jurija v Lovranu' *Muzikološki Zbornik* III (1967) 22–31.

9a. New York, Pierpont Morgan Library, MS M.484, fol. 69r.
    Apocalypse of Margaret of York.

    Date c. 1475.

    Documentation. Otto Pächt *The Master of Mary of Burgundy* (London 1948) pp. 62–3.

10. Amsterdam, Rijksmuseum.
    Adriaen van Wesel *Adoration of the Magi* (fragment of altarpiece).
    Date. 1475–77.

Documentation. W. Vogelsang *Die Holzskulpturen in den Nieder-länder* II (Utrecht 1912) p. 3.

11. Oxford, Saint Hilda's College, Unnumbered MS, fol. 96r.
Flemish Book-of-Hours (Utrecht region).
Date. c. 1475.
Documentation. According to both Dr W. O. Hassall of the Bod-leian Library and the assistant librarian of St Hilda's College, there are no printed references to this manuscript.

12. Budapest, National-Széchényi-Bibliothek, Clmae 424, fol. 3r.
Gradual of King Matthias Corvinus.
Date. 1488–90.
Documentation. J. Balogh *A müvészét Mátyás Kiraly udvárabán* (Budapest 1966) I, 315 ff.; E. Bartoniek *A magyar nemzeti múseum Orszdgos Széchényi könyvtáránatk* I (Budapest 1940) p. 424; E. Berkovits *Illuminated Manuscripts from the Library of Matthias Corvinus* (Budapest 1964) pp. 70–80, 129–30.

12a. Budapest, National-Széchényi-Bibliothek, Clmae 424, fol. 26v.
Gradual of King Matthias Corvinus.
Date. 1488–90.
Documentation. See no. 12 above.

13. Rotterdam, Museum Boymans-van Beuningen.
Geertgen tot Sint Jans *Glorification of the Virgin.*
Date. c. 1489.
Documentation. F. Dühlberg *Niederländische Malerei der Spätgotik* (Potsdam 1929) pp. 96 ff.; H. W. van Us 'Coronatio, Glorificatio en Maria in Sole' *Museum Boymans-van Beuningen Bulletin* XV (1964) 22–38; E. Winternitz 'On angel concerts in the 15th century: a critical approach to realism and symbolism in sacred painting' *The Musical Quarterly* XLIX (1963) 453–6.

14. Urbino, Palazzo Ducale.
Intarsiated Study of Federigo da Montefeltro.
Date. 1479–82.
Documentation. P. Remington 'The Private Study of Federigo da Montefeltro' *Metropolitan Museum of Art Bulletin* XXXVI (1941) 3–13; E. Winternitz 'Quattrocento Science in the Gubbio Studio' *Metropolitan Museum of Art Bulletin* XXXVII (1942) 104 ff.; Ripin, op. cit., pp. 531–2.

14a. Ávila, Museo de la Catedral, Choirbook, fol. Ir.
Choirbook illuminated by Juan de Carrión.
Date. 15th century.
Documentation. None available.

15. Paris, Bibliothèque Nationale, MS fr. 24461, fol. 31r.
Collection of Tapestry Cartoons.
Date. c. 1500.
Documentation. E. Droz and G. Thibault *Poètes et musiciens du XVe*

siècle (Paris 1924) pp. 60, 84; L. de Lincy *Catalogue de la Bibliothèque des ducs de Bourgogne* (Paris 1850) p. 80, Appendix 11; H. Omont *Catalogue générale des manuscrits françaises de la Bibliothèque Nationale* (Paris 1902) pp. 390 ff.; A. Blum 'De l'esprit satirique dans un recueil de "dicts moraux" accompagnés de dessins du xvie siècle' *Mélanges offerts à M. Emile Picot* 11 (Paris 1913) 431–46.

15a. Barcelona, Chapel of the Casa Dalmases.
Antonio Claperós, Carved Angel (sculptured ceiling).
Date. 1400–30.
Documentation. J. M. Lamaña 'Estudio de los instrumentos musicales en los últimos tiempos de la dinastía de la casa de Barcelona' *Miscellanea Barcinonensia* xxi (1969) 21–82 and xxii (1969) 43–64; *Anuario Musical* xxiv (1969) 9–118 (reprint of the preceding); A. Durán y Sanpere, *Sancta María de Cervelló y la calle de Montcado* (Barcelona 1959).

15b. Norfolk, Ranworth Parish Church.
Breviary and Antiphonary (Sarum Use).
Date. c. 1400.
Documentation. London, Courtauld Institute, Photo No. 138/27(36).

15c. London, British Library, ms Add. 22590, fol. 52v.
Book-of-Hours (Flemish).
Date. 1450–70.
Documentation. None.

HARPSICHORD

16. Berlin, Bodemuseum.
Carved Angel in the altarpiece from the Cathedral at Minden.
Date. 1425.
Documentation. Heyde, op. cit., pp. 33–4.

17. Paris, Bibliothèque Nationale, ms lat. 7295, fol. 128r.
Henri Arnaut de Zwolle *Pro composicione clavisimbali.*
Date. 1436–54.
Documentation. See no. 4 above; and E. A. Bowles 'On the origin of the keyboard mechanism in the Late Middle Ages' *Technology and Culture* vii (1966) esp. pp. 160 ff.

18. Warwick, Saint Mary's Church.
John Prudd, Musician-Angel (stained-glass window, Beauchamp Chapel).
Date. 1439–47.
Documentation. See no. 5 above.

19. Manchester Cathedral.
Carved Musician-Angel (wooden corbel at nave ceiling).
Date. 1465–68.

Documentation. J. S. Crowther *Architectural History of Manchester Cathedral* (Manchester 1894); H. A. Hudson *The Medieval Woodwork of Manchester Cathedral* (Manchester 1924) esp. pp. 162 f.; H. A. Hudson *The Minstrel Angels of Manchester Cathedral* (St Annes-on-Sea 1922) pp. 14 f.

20. Paris, Bibliothèque Nationale, MS fr. 331, fol. 145v.
    Guillaume Fillastre *Istoire de la conqueste du noble et riche thoison d'or.*
    Date. 1468.
    Documentation. G. Doutrepont *La litterature française à la cour des ducs de Bourgogne* (Paris 1909) pp. 161 f.; A. Pirro *Les clavecinistes* (Paris 1930) p. 11; B. Woledge *Bibliographie des romans et nouvelles en prose française antérieurs à 1500* (Geneva 1954) p. 104.

21. Uppland, Sånga Church.
    Musician-Angel (fresco).
    Date. c. 1470.
    Documentation. Hellquist, op. cit.

22. Lovran, Saint George's Church.
    Musician-Angel (fresco on presbytery vault).
    Date. 1470–79.
    Documentation. See no. 9 above.

23. Uppland, Häverö Church.
    Musician-Angel (fresco).
    Date. c. 1475.
    Documentation. Norlind, op. cit., pp. 48, 245, 248; Hellquist, op. cit.

24. Paris, Bibliothèque Nationale, MS fr. 1673, fol. 1r.
    Ymbert Chandelier *Enseignements à Madame d'Angoulesme.*
    Date. 1483.
    Documentation. L. V. Delisle *Catalogue des manuscrits français de la Bibliothèque Impériale* I (Paris 1868) p. 285; Pirro, op. cit., p. 7.

25. Chantilly, Musée Condé, MS lat. 1284, fol. 126.
    Pol de Limbourg and Jean Colombe *Très Riches Heures du Duc de Berry.*
    Date. 1486.
    Documentation. P. Durrieu *Les très riches heures de Jean de France* (Paris 1904) esp. pp. 106–13; J. Meurgey *Les principaux manuscrits à peintures du Musée Condé à Chantilly* (Paris 1930) pp. 59–71

26. March, Saint Wendreda's Church.
    Carved Musician-Angel (base of wall-post between clerestory windows).
    Date. Before 1500.
    Documentation. A. C. Turnbull *The Parish Church of Saint Wendreda,* rev. ed. (Peterborough 1966) esp. pp. 6 f.; N. Pevsner *Cambridgeshire* (Harmondsworth 1954) pp. 345 f.

27. Uppland, Jumkil Church.
    Musician-Angel (fresco).

Date. c. 1500.
Documentation. Norlind, op. cit., pp. 48, 245, 247; Hellquist, op. cit.
27a. New York, Pierpont Morgan Library, MS M834, fol. 25.
Book-of-Hours (Fouquet Workshop).
Date. 1475–90.
Documentation. H. Martin *Les Fouquet de Chantilly* (Paris 1926);
K. G. Perls *Jean Fouquet* (London/New York 1940);
P. Wescher *Fouquet und seine Zeit* (Basel 1945).
27b. Mishimo, Okano Collection, Unnumbered MS fol. 1.
Antiphonal (Spanish).
Date. c. 1480.
Documentation. Maggs Musical Miscellany No. 1 (April 1975) 16.

VARIANT FORMS
28. Paris, Bibliothèque Nationale, MS lat. 7295, fol. 129v.
Henri Arnaut de Zwolle *Pro composicione instrumenti vocati
dulce melos.*
Date. 1436–54.
Documentation. See no. 4 above.
29. Paris, Bibliothèque Nationale, MS lat. 7295, fol. 130r.
Henri Arnaut de Zwolle *Alter modus ponendi stephanos.*
Date. 1436–54.
Documentation. See no. 4 above.
30. Cambridge, Fitzwilliam Museum, MS 25, fol. 23v.
Ludolphus of Saxony *Life of Christ.*
Date. c. 1470.
Documentation. A. W. Byvanck *La miniature dans les Pays-Bas septen-
trionaux* (Paris 1937) pp. 102, 127; A. W. Byvanck and
G. J. Hoogewerff *La miniature hollandaise* (Paris 1922) p. 56;
M. R. James *Descriptive Catalogue of the Manuscripts in the Fitz-
william Museum* (Cambridge 1895).
31. Kefermarkt, Saint Wolfgang's Church.
Carved Musician-Angel (wooden base of statue of patron saint).
Date. 1490–97.
Documentation. S. Kruckenhauser *Das Meisterwerk von Kefermarkt*
(Salzburg 1942); F. Oberchristl *Der gotischer Flügaltar und die
Kirche zu Kefermarkt* (Linz 1904); F. Oberchristl *Kefermarkt
und sein gotischer Flügaltar* (Linz 1926).
31a. Malvern, *ex coll.* Dyson Perrins, Unnumbered MS fol. 38r.
Book-of-Hours (Tours).
Date. c. 1450.
Documentation. Sotheby's Sale Catalog 1 December 1959, Lot 85;
Courtauld Institute Photo No. 271/55(28a).

NOTE

Six familiar examples commonly assigned to the fifteenth century, and excluded from this checklist, should be mentioned: (1) a clavichord and (2) a harpsichord illustrated in Weimar, Thüringische Landesbibliothek, *Ingenieurkunst- und Wunderbuch*, fol. 328. Although there is much contradictory information on when this was produced (it is a product of several hands), it is definitely not fifteenth-century — more likely *c.* 1510. The labels referred to by James in *Early Keyboard Instruments* p. 92, are not to be found in the manuscript itself, and in fact the two representations have no text associated with them. (3) a clavicytherium depicted in a Ghent University Library manuscript 'of about 1450'. This example is discussed and illustrated in van der Straeten *La musique au pays-bas avant le 19e siècle* I, pp. 278 f. As he himself noted, two manuscripts bound together with the one containing the drawing of the clavicytherium are dated 1503 and 1504. Despite his speculation to the contrary, there seems to be no reason for assuming that the undated treatise with the keyboard instrument is any earlier. (4) A keyed psaltery depicted in a statue of King David in the Carthusian Monastery at Pavia. Based upon the statement of Ambros *Geschichte der Musik* II, 505 (addendum to p. 200), Neupert and others have cited a trapezoidal instrument 'with eight keys', which David operates with his right hand. An examination of detailed photographs recently taken for the author reveals the instrument to be an ordinary psaltery played with a plectrum. (The relief sculpture is on the left façade of the Certosa, and not in a basement niche as Ambros stated.) (5) A harpsichord and (6) a variant form, spinet-like, found on an intarsiated choir stall from the Cathedral of San Lorenzo in Genoa. According to P. Torriti, 'Le tarsie del coro di San Lorenzo in Genova' *Bollettino Linguistico* VI (1955) 71–96, these artifacts should be dated between 1514 and 1530.

In addition, one further example is omitted for want of sufficient information in the single source that mentions it, F. W. Galpin's article 'Musical instruments' in Percy Macquoid *Dictionary of English Furniture*, rev. ed. by R. Edwards (London 1954) II, 372. Galpin states that a fifteenth-century Sarum Breviary contains a representation of a clavichord similar to that shown in the Shrewsbury sculpture (no. 3 above) 'but with twelve keys'.

Finally, although Pirro *Les Clavecinistes*, p. 7, states that Paris, Bibliothèque Nationale, MS fr. 1763 shows 'un clavichorde rectangulaire' in addition to the harpsichord cited as no. 24 above, no such representation is actually to be found in the manuscript.

1

Clavichord. German, anon., 1425. *Staatliche Museen zu Berlin*

Clavichord. Italian, Leonardo da Besozzo and Perrineto da Benevento, soon after 1433. *Gabinetto Fotografico Nazionale, Rome*

2

3

Clavichord. English, anon., *c.* 1440. *National
Buildings Record, London*

4▶

Clavichord. English, John Prudd, 1439–47.
National Buildings Record, London

5

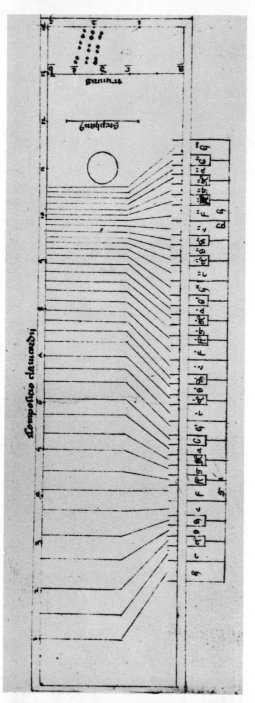

4

Clavichord. Burgundian, Henri Arnaut de Zwolle,
1436–54. *Bibliothèque Nationale, Paris*

Clavichord. German. Heinrich Czun, 1448. *Franz
Höch, Coburg*

Pedal clavichord. German, anon., after 1467.
Württembergische Landesbibliothek, Stuttgart

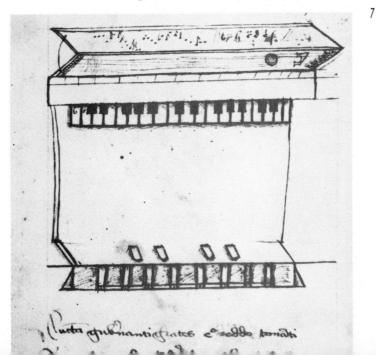

8

Clavichord. Swedish, anon., *c.* 1470. *Per-Anders Hellquist, Stockholm*

Clavichord. Istrian, anon., 1470–9. *Regionalni Zavod za Zaštitu Spomenika Kulture, Rijeka*

9

9a

Clavichord. Flemish, Master of Mary of Burgundy,
c. 1475. *Pierpont Morgan Library, New York*

10a

Clavichord. Dutch, Adriaen van Wesel, 1475–7.
Rijksmuseum, Amsterdam

Clavichord. (Top view of instrument shown in
plate 10a.) *Rijksmuseum, Amsterdam*

11

Clavichord. Flemish, anon., *c.* 1475. *St Hilda's College, Oxford*

Clavichord. French, anon., 1488–90. *National-Széchényi-Bibliothek, Budapest*

12

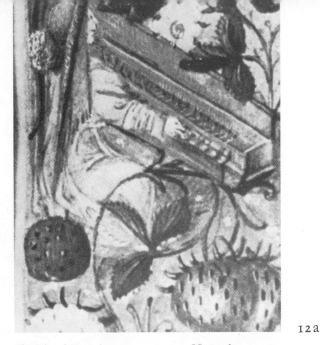

12a

Clavichord. French, anon., 1488–90. *National-Széchényi-Bibliothek, Budapest*

Clavichord. Dutch, Geertgen tot Sint Jans, *c.* 1489. *Museum Boymans-van Beuningen, Rotterdam*

13

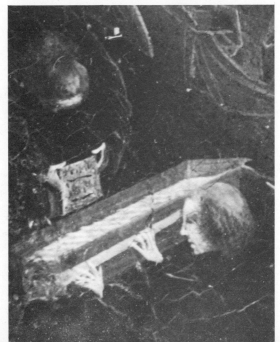

14

Clavichord. Italian, anon., 1479–82. *Soprentendenza
alle Gallerie delle Marche, Urbino*

14a

Clavichord. Spanish, Juan de Carrión, 15th century. *Museo de la Catedral, Ávila*

15 ▶

Harpsichord. German, anon., 1425. *Staatliche Museen zu Berlin*

16

15

Clavichord. French, anon., before 1500.
Bibliothèque Nationale, Paris

15 a

Clavichord. Spanish, Antonio Claperós, 1400–30.
Anuario Musical, Barcelona

15 b

Clavichord. English, anon., *c.* 1400.
Courtauld Institute, London

15 C

Clavichord. Flemish, anon., 1450-70. *British Library, London*

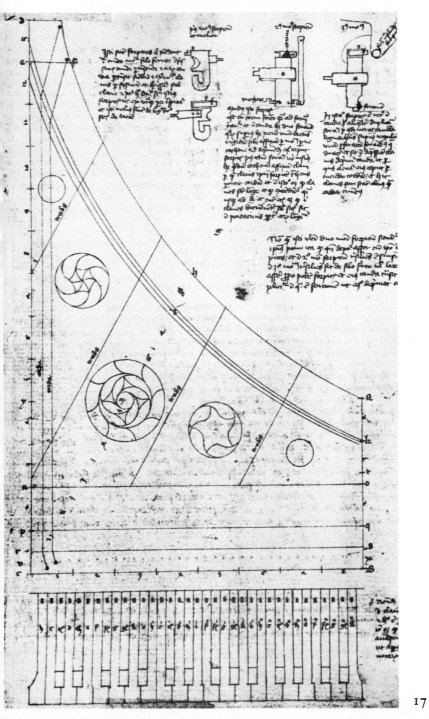

Harpsichord. Burgundian, Henri Arnaut de Zwolle, 1436–54. *Bibliothèque Nationale, Paris*

17

18

Harpsichord. English, John Prudd, 1439–47.
National Buildings Record, London

Harpsichord. English, anon., 1465–8. *Pitkin Pictorials, Ltd., London*

19

20

Harpsichord. French, Guillaume Fillastre, 1468.
Bibliothèque Nationale, Paris

Harpsichord. Swedish, anon., *c.* 1470.
Per-Anders Hellquist, Stockholm

21

22

Harpsichord. Istrian, anon., 1470–9. *Regionalni
Zavod za Zaštitu Spomenika Kulture, Rijeka*

23

Harpsichord. Swedish, anon., *c*. 1475. *Per-Anders Hellquist, Stockholm*

Harpsichord. French, Ymbert Chandelier, 1483. *Bibliothèque Nationale, Paris*

24

25

Harpsichord. French, Jean de Colombe, 1486.
Giraudon, Paris

26

Harpsichord. English, anon., before 1500

27

Harpsichord. Swedish, anon., *c.* 1500.
Per-Anders Hellquist, Stockholm

27 a

Harpsichord. French, Fouquet Workshop, 1475–90.
Pierpont Morgan Library, New York

Harpsichord. Spanish, anon., *c.* 1480.
Maggs Bros. Ltd., London

27 b

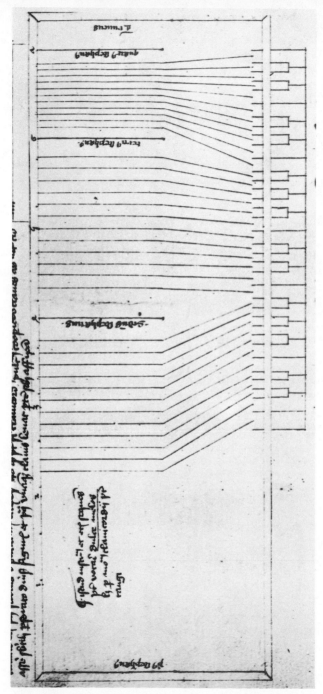

28

Dulce melos. Burgundian, Henri Arnaut de Zwolle,
1436–54. *Bibliothèque Nationale, Paris*

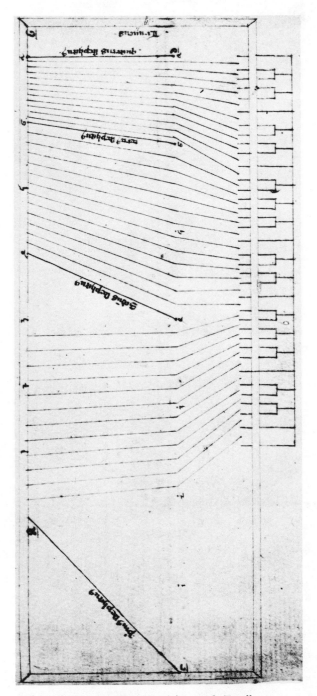

Dulce melos. Burgundian, Henri Arnaut de Zwolle,
1436–54. *Bibliothèque Nationale, Paris*

29

 30

Wing-shaped clavichord. Dutch, anon., *c.* 1470.
Fitzwilliam Museum, Cambridge

Clavicytherium. Austrian, anon., 1490–7

31

I a

Keyed Psaltery. French, anon., *c.* 1450.
Courtauld Institute, London

The Truchado Instrument: a Geigenwerk?

F. J. DE HEN
Professor of Musicology, State University of Ghent

In 1902, the Musical Instrument Museum of the Royal Conservatory in Brussels acquired an instrument bought in Spain and bearing the inscription FRAY RAYMUNDO TRUCHADO : INVENTOR· 1625 (plate 32). Since no appropriate Spanish name was known and because of its resemblance to an instrument depicted by Praetorius,[1] the author of the Museum's catalogue,[2] Victor-Charles Mahillon, called this instrument a geigenwerk. Ever since its arrival in the Museum, the Truchado instrument has been the cause of hot discussions regarding its name, its origin, and even its authenticity.

In 1966, the instrument was restored by the firm of Knud Kaufmann and Son in Brussels. Prior to this, it had been in several hands, and a number of inscriptions were found inside the case: 'Feliz Sanchez en 30 d marzo año de 1765'; 'Manuel Revez restaurado en Madrid 1892'; and 'Schockaert 1902'. (Schockaert was the apprentice of Fr de Vestibule, who restored the instrument under Mahillon's supervision.) In addition, F. Moisse worked on the instrument at some time prior to 1958, and in 1959 Jacques Bernard in Liège repaired a few cracks in the soundboard.

The general appearance of the instrument is that of a very rough and clumsily made harpsichord. Its shape is not at all that of a 'pig's head'[3] but, rather, reminds one of the muslim *q'anūn*, though much bigger, deeper, and heavier. Unlike those of a harpsichord, all five sides of the Truchado instrument are straight. The instrument is 1510 mm (59.4) long, 860 mm (33.9) wide, and 430 mm (16.9) deep. The low stand is 255 mm. (10) high.

The interior of the lid is ornamented with two paintings (plate 33). The one on the front panel shows a nymph being abducted by tritons, with Cupid hovering above them. The triangular back panel shows a palace with its garden. Winternitz[4] has suggested that the back panel was cut down from a rectangular painting and that the two panels are so different in style that they cannot be assumed to have been originally part of the instrument. However, the cover is not composed of two separate pieces, both paintings having been executed on a single panel (plate 33a). The coniferous wood of this panel and the gypsum preparation that underlies the paint suggest a southern origin for the paintings. An outside covering of red silk was removed in the recent restoration. The wood of the case under this silk was found to have been painted in imitation of green marble. However, this paint cannot be original, since there is a layer of brown paint beneath it and since the green paint covers the puttying-over of traces of earlier hinges.[5] The coat of arms embroidered on the silk covering, which might give a clue to the provenance of the instrument, has yet to be identified, although several elements in it point to Madrid as its place of origin.

The keyboard, which is set within the case and completely covered by the wrestplank, has a compass of four octaves C/E–c''', the lowest octave being short. The naturals are covered with boxwood; the wooden accidentals are stained black. The fronts of the keys are decorated with a composite arcade similar to that used in Italian harpsichords, and the accidentals are decorated with transversely scored lines. The span for three octaves (*stichmass*) is relatively small, 483 mm (19.0) compared to that on other instruments of the period, which generally falls between 490 and 510 mm (19.3–20.1).

The action of the instrument is complex. Turning a crank set in the tail imparts a rotary movement to a thick beam, quadrangular in cross section, that runs under the soundboard parallel to the spine. The other end of this beam pierces four driving wheels of different diameters (plate 34). Leather belts transmit the rotation of the driving wheels to four friction wheels that protrude through the soundboard under the strings so that the strings can be brought into contact with them. Owing to the different diameters of the driving wheels, the speed of rotation is different for each friction wheel : the first, which serves the bass strings, rotates at the same rate as the crank; the fourth, which serves the treble strings, turns two and a half times as fast. The two friction wheels at the left turn in the opposite direction from those at the right. The strings are fixed along the side and the tail of the instrument on a rather thick hitchpin rail (figure 1). The thick iron tuning pins are set in a wrestplank that is placed directly over the keyboard. The upper surface of the wrestplank is shaped to match the contour of the four friction wheels but is slightly higher, so that the strings pass over the wheels without touching them. Two arcaded pieces of wood about 25 mm (1.0) thick are set between the wrestplank and the friction wheels. A thin brass rod set into the more distant of these pieces (that nearer the friction wheels) acts as a nut. An iron rod running parallel to each string is mounted on these transverse pieces by means of eyelets. The ends of these rods are bent at right angles to the central part, the near end being formed into a loop and the far end into a fork (figure 2). When one depresses a key, a wire attached to the key in front of the balance rail and passing through the wrestplank, pulls down on the near end of the rod; the other end, with its fork grasping the string, pulls the string down-

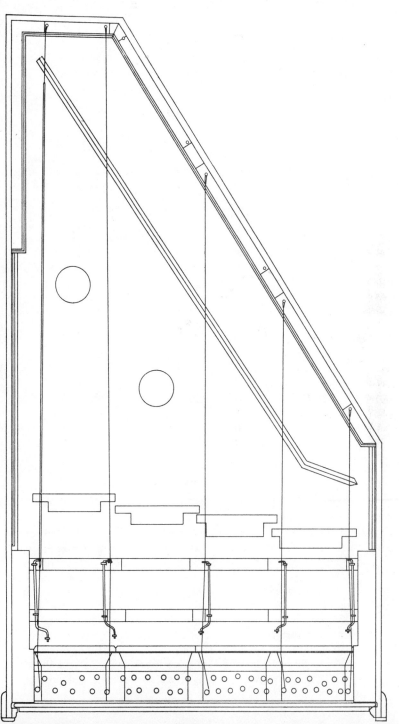

Figure 1

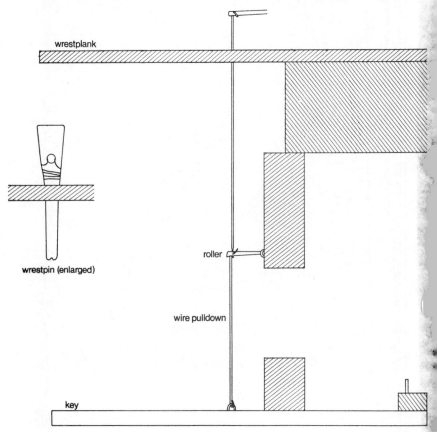

wrestplank

wrestpin (enlarged)

roller

wire pulldown

key

Figure 2

ward, bringing it into contact with the turning friction wheel, which sets the string into vibration. As soon as the key is released, the tension of the string restores the iron rod to its initial position and the string stops vibrating. There is no damper mechanism. Since the arrangement of the strings does not always permit them to lie directly above the corresponding keys, several of the wire pulldowns are interrupted by short iron rollers attached to a board below the wrestplank. Two of these rollers, which are somewhat longer than the others, make it possible for the D/F♯ key to actuate the second string and the E/G♯ key the third, so that, the short-octave keyboard notwithstanding, the strings are tuned in ascending order.

The four friction wheels are mounted on a crossbar that runs parallel to the belly rail. They are 180 mm (7.1) in diameter and are made of a tin-antimony alloy, and their rubbing surfaces are covered with a layer of cloth, followed by a very thin layer of wood and finally a layer of parchment. The strings are unequally allotted to the four wheels. The first, which rotates most slowly, serves the 9 lowest strings; the second serves the next 11 strings; the third the next 12 strings; and the fourth, which rotates most rapidly, the highest 13 strings. The driving wheels are made of wood and the grooves for the belts that connect them to the friction wheels are equipped with nails to eliminate slippage. These nails are unnecessary with the existing leather belts and suggest that the original belts may have been made of cord.

When Truchado's instrument arrived at the Museum, it was strung with gut. However, marks left on the nut reveal that it was once strung with brass or iron wire, and the tapered scaling (see below) makes it most probable that iron wire was used. Presumably in the last quarter of the nineteenth century, the gut strings were introduced and the original tuning pins were replaced. That the existing tuning pins are of recent make is proved by the structural analysis of the metal.[6] Wooden plugs in the wrestplank prove the existence of previous thicker, probably wooden pins. The use of gut for stringing can be much older. In the eighteenth century it was still in use for harpsichords;[7] Hans Haiden, who built the geigenwerk pictured by Praetorius, started with gut, changed to wire,[8] and changed back again. Ernest Closson[9] suggested that metal strings might be presumed to give an inferior sound, but this is not entirely true. Kaufmann and Son during the 1966 restoration tried all kinds of strings, for example gut, steel, brass, even phosphor bronze wire, and over-spinning with silk and parchment. Of all these experiments, only steel strings (overspun with parchment in the bass as described by Praetorius)[10] gave a really satisfactory sound. An additional reason for the use of metal instead of gut strings is provided by the fact that if gut strings are used, their tension is insufficient to lift the keys when they are released. For this reason, a small wooden rail with Pleyel grand piano springs had been placed under the keys. (During the last restoration this was, of course, removed.) This seems to prove that gut strings were not original and that the mechanism was conceived in terms of metal strings.

Neither Spain nor Portugal appears to have had a strong tradition of harpsichord-making in the early seventeenth century.[11] Accordingly, one might expect Truchado to have been experimenting with strings and scaling. The scaling of his instrument is relatively short and strongly tapered.

c′′′	172 mm	6.8 inches
c′′	278	10.9
c′	522	20.6
c	840	33.1
C/E	1048	41.3

A tapered scale is more in the line of the Flemish school of harpsichord-makers,[12] and it is not impossible that they left their mark indirectly on the Truchado instrument, since Flemish instruments were well known in Spain in the sixteenth and seventeenth centuries.

The soundboard is not original and has been replaced at least twice, once when the instrument arrived at the Museum and again during the 1966 restoration. According to Mahillon and Closson, the soundboard was copied exactly in the earlier restoration. It was decorated with water-colour paintings of flowers and birds like those on the soundboard of a Flemish harpsichord; however, instead of a single soundhole and a pewter rose, there are two soundholes, one of which still retains a gilded parchment rose. The present soundboard is 5 mm (0.2) thick at the soundholes and is slightly tapered. It rests on a solid 40 × 35 mm (1.6 × 1.4) lining. No evidence has survived regarding the original barring or ribbing. As the instrument is restored now, there is no cut-off bar. The arcaded bridge has a total length of 1165 mm (45.9). Its maximum width is 16.8 mm (0.7), its minimum width is 15.5 mm (0.6) its maximum height is 62 mm (2.4), and its minimum height is 27 mm (1.1).

A comparison of the organological features of the Truchado instrument and Haiden's geigenwerk as depicted by Praetorius shows that the Truchado instrument is not merely a copy, although it was certainly influenced by Haiden's, an example of which is known to have been owned by the Spanish royal family.[13] To begin with, the Truchado instrument is not shaped like a normal harpsichord, and its keyboard does not project like that on Haiden's geigenwerk. Instead of driving the friction wheels with one or more pedals, Truchado used a crank, which has to be turned by a helper while the performer plays at the keyboard. Praetorius' drawing appears to show some sort of damper mechanism, which is lacking on the Truchado instrument. Finally, the instrument is so low that one must squat on the floor to play it. It has been suggested that this may be due to Moorish influence. Although no alternative explanation suggests itself, it hardly seems believable that a Spanish monk in the seventeenth century would adhere to infidels' habits. The instrument cannot, incidentally, be placed on a table as Haiden's could, since its keyboard is then too high for comfortable playing.

Hans Haiden gives an impressive list of the musical possibilities of his geigenwerk in the *Musicale instrumentum reformatum*,[14] including its ability to achieve dynamic variation and vibrato, to bring out one part against a chord, to sustain tones indefinitely, to vary the tempo at will, to produce echo effects, and to imitate the lute, bagpipe, hurdy-gurdy, cittern, viola bastarda, and (with the aid of a drum stop) military music. An attempt to find these resources in the Truchado instrument meets with only mixed success. Its tone is nasal, especially in the treble, and the instrument is well suited for accompanying voices or wind instruments. Within a very small range, differences in loudness can be achieved, thereby making it possible to produce limited echo effects. Tempo changes are, of course, possible, but rapid runs and such embellishments as trills are to be avoided. A lute cannot be imitated, and staccato playing is almost impossible. A single part cannot be brought out against a chord; on the other hand, vibrato (although difficult to produce) is possible. Both the hurdy-gurdy and bagpipe can readily be imitated owing to the ease of obtaining drone effects. However, neither cittern music nor band music can even be approximated, and only a very charitable critic would claim a close imitation of the viola bastarda.

One final point to consider is the instrument's inscription. Nothing whatever is known about the maker, although Closson[15] has made the plausible suggestion that 'Truchado' means 'of Truchas', a village in the province of Leon in northwest Spain. The foregoing discussion makes it clear that Truchado was not the actual inventor of instruments of this type. 'Inventor' can, of course, mean 'designer' or even merely 'maker'. Although it is possible that Truchado made some improvements on an experimental instrument of some kind, his instrument is clearly more primitive than Haiden's developed examples. Experiments in this area can be traced back at least as far as Leonardo da Vinci's time[16] and are, of course, ultimately traceable to the hurdy-gurdy or organistrum. It seems probable, as Georg Kinsky[17] has stated, that Haiden's point of departure was the instrument equipped with a 'matassa' mentioned by Galilei.[18]

Stringing of the Truchado Instrument

The strings for C/E–e are steel covered with parchment;
the higher strings are plain steel.

NOTE	VIBRATING LENGTH		DIAMETER		NOTE	VIBRATING LENGTH		DIAMETER	
	mm	*inches*	*mm*	*inches*		*mm*	*inches*	*mm*	*inches*
C/E	1048	41.26	2.94	.116	e′	458	18.02	0.40	.016
D	1018	40.08	2.60	.102	f′	434	17.08	0.40	.016
E	991	39.02	2.57	.101	f#′	417	16.42	0.40	.016
F	965	37.99	2.26	.089	g′	395	15.55	0.40	.016
G	940	37.00	2.60	.102	g#′	370	14.57	0.40	.016
A	910	35.83	2.25	.089	a′	356	14.02	0.40	.016
B♭	886	34.88	1.90	.075	b♭′	340	13.38	0.40	.016
B	863	33.98	2.10	.083	b′	328	12.91	0.40	.016
c	840	33.07	1.66	.065	c″	278	10.94	0.40	.016
c#	785	30.90	1.80	.071	c#″	261	10.28	0.40	.016
d	767	30.20	1.63	.064	d″	250	9.84	0.40	.016
e♭	745	29.33	1.20	.047	e♭″	234	9.21	0.40	.016
e	723	28.46	0.75	.030	e″	210	8.27	0.40	.016
f	701	27.60	0.70	.028	f″	198	7.80	0.40	.016
f#	684	26.93	0.65	.026	f#″	193	7.60	0.40	.016
g	657	25.87	0.65	.026	g″	190	7.48	0.40	.016
g#	630	24.80	0.60	.024	g#″	186	7.32	0.35	.014
a	612	24.09	0.55	.022	a″	182	7.17	0.35	.014
b♭	596	23.46	0.50	.020	b♭″	177	6.97	0.35	.014
b	585	23.03	0.50	.020	b″	174	6.85	0.35	.014
c′	522	20.55	0.45	.018	c‴	172	6.77	0.35	.014
c#′	510	20.08	0.45	.018					
d′	492	19.37	0.45	.018					
e♭′	477	18.78	0.40	.016					

NOTES AND REFERENCES

1   M. Praetorius *Syntagma musicum* II (Wolfenbüttel 1619) plate III.
2   V.-Ch. Mahillon *Catalogue descriptif et analytique du Musée Instrumental du Conservatoire Royal de Musique de Bruxelles* IV (Ghent 1912) pp. 286 ff.
3   Praetorius, op. cit., p. 63.
4   E. Winternitz *Musical Instruments of the Western World* (New York 1966) p. 108.
5   ACL Report 2L/43/195.240/RL/MD.
6   ACL Report 2L/43/490.591/RL/MD. The tuning pins are 99 mm (3.90) long and have an average diameter of 10 mm (0.39). They were formed by cold-hammering, as shown by the deformation of the grain of the metal. This proves that the holes for the strings must have been drilled. As a result, one may conclude that the tuning pins date from the first half of the nineteenth century at the earliest.
7   See F. Hubbard *Three Centuries of Harpsichord Making* (Cambridge, Mass., 1965) pp. 327–30.
8   H. Haiden *Commentario de musicali instrumento* (Nürnberg 1605) p. 42: '…non ovinis chordis, …sed chalybcis atque orichalceis fidibus inducatur hoc nostrum instrumentum.…' ('Our instrument is strung not with sheep gut but with steel or brass strings'). Id., *Musicale instrumentum reformatum* (Nürnberg 1610) p. 30: 'es ist auch umb soviel desto annemlicher weil est nicht soviel stimmen darff als Lauten oder Geigen von wegen die Saitten nicht schäfen, sondern alle von Messing und Eysen sind welche durch langen Gebrauch je langer je besser werden und sich nicht bald verstimmen.' ('it is also so much more acceptable because it does not need to be tuned so much as lutes or violins, owing to the fact that the strings are not made of sheep gut but entirely of brass and iron, which in long use grow better the longer they are used and will not quickly get out of tune.').
9   E. Closson 'Le geigenwerk au Musée du Conservatoire de Bruxelles' *Le Guide Musical* L (1904) 356.
10 Op. cit., p. 68.
11 F. J. Hirt *Meisterwerke des Klavierbaus* (Olten 1955) p. 501, gives 1703 as the earliest evidence for Portugal and 1800 for Spain. This is confirmed by M. S. Kastner, who in a letter to the Museum states that if Spanish-made harpsichords existed in the sixteenth and seventeenth centuries, no traces remain today. On the other hand, D. H. Boalch *Makers of the Harpsichord and Clavichord* (London 1956) p. 87, and R. Russell *The Harpsichord and Clavichord* (London 1959) p. 115, cite an inventory of 1583 reprinted by E. van der Straeten *La musique aux Pays-Bas avant le 19e siècle* II (Brussels 1872) p. 312, that includes 'Un clavicordio grande con dos juegos que se compro de Juan Bautista Quebon'. However, this text does not specifically state that Quebon built the harpsichord in question.
12 W. R. Thomas and J. J. K. Rhodes 'The string scales of Italian keyboard instruments' *Galpin Society Journal* XX (1967) 52–4.
13 Van der Straeten, op. cit., VIII (Brussels 1888) p. 302, quotes an account of 1872 that mentions a *'violicembalo*, a kind of bowed harpsichord invented by Johann Heyden of Nürnberg' then at the Escorial and said to have been brought there at the order of Philip III (r. 1598–1621).

14   P. 14; reprinted by Praetorius, op. cit., pp. 69–71.

15   Op. cit., p. 379.

16   See E. Winternitz 'Leonardo's invention of the viola organista'
      Raccolta Vinciana fasc. xx (1964).

17   G. Kinsky 'Hans Haiden, der Erfinder der Nürnbergischen Gei-
      genwerks', *Zeitschrift für Musikwissenschaft* vi (Jan.–Feb. 1924)
      201.

18   V. Galilei *Della Musica antica e della moderna* (Florence 1581) p. 48;
      'Vn'altroessempio d'uno Strumento di tasti, che già l'Elettore
      Augusto Duca di Sassonia, donò alla felice memoria del Grande
      Alberto di Baueria, mi sovviene ni questo proposito, più di cias-
      cuno altro efficace. il quale Strumento ha le corde secondo l'vso di
      quelle del Liuto, & vengano secate à guisa di quelle della Viola da
      vn'accomodata matassa artificiosamente fatta delle medesime setole
      di che si fanno le corde à gli archi delle Viole : la qual matassa con
      assai facilità, viene menata in giro con vn piede da quello istesso
      che lo suona, & ne seca continuamente col mezzo d'vna ruota
      sopra la quale passa, quella quantita che vogliano le dita di lui.'
      ('Another example of a keyboard instrument, which at that time
      the Elector Augustus, Duke of Saxony, gave in loving memory of
      the great Albert of Bavaria, comes to mind in this connection as
      being more efficient than any other. This instrument has strings
      similar to those of the lute, and they are stroked, in the manner of
      those of the viol, by a skein of appropriate shape artfully made of
      the same hairs used to make the strings of viol bows. This skein is
      very easily turned by the foot of the player himself, and it strokes
      [the strings] continuously, by means of a wheel over which it
      passes, to the degree that his fingers demand.')

32

The Truchado instrument (Musée Instrumental de Bruxelles). *A.C.L.*, Brussels

Paintings on the lid of the Truchado
instrument. *A.C.L., Brussels*

33 a

The lid after repair and with the cloth covering
removed. *A.C.L., Brussels*

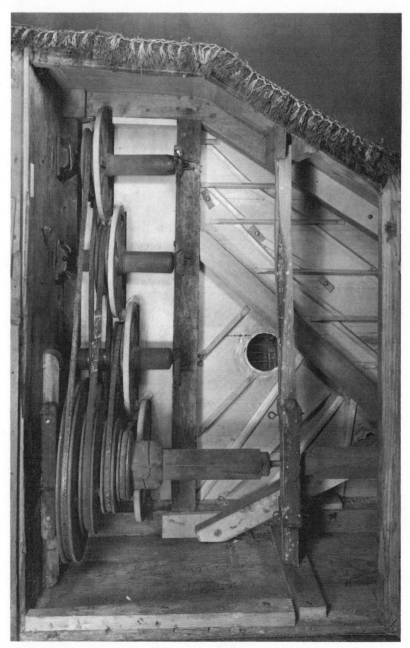

34

Drive wheels and friction wheels of the Truchado
instrument. *A.C.L., Brussels*

The Single-strung Italian Harpsichord

FRIEDEMANN HELLWIG
Oberrestaurator, Germanisches Nationalmuseum, Nuremberg

The more we come to know of Italian harpsichord-making, the more we become aware of the fact that *the* Italian harpsichord does not exist. In recent years, many interesting details have been discovered that do not fit into the conception of a single Italian harpsichord standard, surviving virtually unchanged for three centuries. The aim of this essay, inspired by the restoration of a 1577 Bertarini harpsichord, is to contribute to the knowledge of one special Italian type.

It is probably owing to their simple disposition that very little attention has been paid to single-strung harpsichords, although at least eight instruments of this kind have been preserved. These are enumerated in the following list, and their characteristics are summarized in the table overleaf:[1]

1. Anonymous (name of maker illegible), Italy, 1503. Milan, Museo Civico. (The instrument has been converted to a clavichord by replacing the jacks with tangents.)[2]

2. Hieronymus Bononiensis 1521. London, Victoria and Albert Museum. (The instrument now possesses two 8' registers, but according to the Museum's catalogue, it originally had only one.)[3]

3. Dominicus Pisaurensis 1533. Leipzig, Musical Instrument Museum of the Karl-Marx-Universität.[4]

4. Ioannes Baptista Bertarinus, Rome, 1577. Florence, Museo Bardini. (There are some doubts as to the authenticity of the inscription on the jack rail; however, the initials 'GB' on the keys appear to be original.)[5]

5. Anonymous, Italy (Florence?), 16th century. Nürnberg, Germanisches Nationalmuseum (Rück Collection).[6]

6. Anonymous, Italy, 16th or 17th century. London, Fenton House (Benton Fletcher Collection.).[7]

7. Giovanni Battista Boni 1619. Brussels, Musical Instrument Museum of the Conservatoire Royal de Musique.[8]

8. Anonymous, Italy, early 17th century. Olveston, Bristol, A.C.N.Mackenzie of Ord.[9]

All these instruments were made in Italy, and no single-strung harpsichord made elsewhere has survived.[10] Although such instruments are generally considered to be a phenomenon of the sixteenth century,[11] the dates of those listed above do not completely

Characteristics of the Instruments Listed

Maker	Date	Length mm	inches	Original compass	Scaling[a] mm	inches
Anonymous	1503	1760	69.3	C/E–c'''	267	10.5
Hieronymus Bononiensis	1521	1800	70.9	C/E–c''' or F–f'''	267[b]	10.5[b]
Dominicus Pisaurensis	1533	1830	72.0	C/E–f'''	288	11.3
I.B. Bertarinus	1577	1790	70.5	C/E–c'''	295	11.6
Anonymous	16th c.	1910	75.2	C/E–c'''	275	10.8
Anonymous	16th or 17th c.	1855	73.0	C/E–c'''	288	11.3
G.B. Boni	1619	1930	76.0	C/E–c'''	262	10.3
Anonymous	early 17th c.	1916	75.4	FF(?)–c'''	275	10.8

[a] Sounding length of c''.
[b] Sounding length of the longer c'' string in the present C/E–d''' compass.

accord with this view. There is even evidence for the assertion that single-strung instruments were made as late as *c.* 1700, since four such harpsichords made by Cristofori are listed in an inventory of 1713, prepared when he took charge of the instruments of Cosimo III, Grand Duke of Tuscany.[12] In view of the fact that such harpsichords appear to have been built throughout the better part of two centuries, an evolutionary explanation of the single-strung instrument in terms of its representing the earliest form of Italian harpsichord seems unjustified. It is not proper to consider such instruments as spinets (as Hirt[13] claims, on the ground that both are single-strung — as indeed they are), nor is there any sound evidence that in harpsichord-making single stringing preceded double stringing, since double stringing is mentioned by Arnault of Zwolle in the mid-1400s.

All but one of the instruments listed above are of true inner-outer construction, although only a few preserve their original outer cases. Of these, the Hieronymus Bononiensis and the Nürnberg Collection's anonymous instrument call for special attention because their cases are covered with leather tooled and gilt with ornamental designs. The case of the anonymous instrument (plate 35) seems to be the older of the two, since it dates from the sixteenth century. Its sides are covered with architectural ornaments showing arcades with lions carrying alternately lilies and roses (plate 36). This use of the lion with a lily points to the instrument's having been built in Florence, a suggestion that is supported by the discovery of a Florentine coin under the leather covering during the restoration. The instrument rests on an original gilt stand.

Four of the eight instruments listed are made of cypress, the exceptions being the Dominicus Pisaurensis (plates 37 and 38), which is made of cedar, the Bertarinus (plates 39 and 40) and the Nürnberg anonymous, the sides of which are maple, and the Bristol anonymous, which is of false inner-outer construction but has a cypress-lined case. (The use of maple seems to be an early feature, dating from a period during which Italian harpsichord-making was not yet as standardized as in the following centuries.) In size, all the instruments belong to the smaller type, their lengths ranging from 1790 mm (70.5) to 1920 mm (75.4). However, two of the instruments (the Hieronymus Bononiensis and the Dominicus Pisaurensis) do not have the long slanting tail that is generally considered to be characteristic of all early Italian harpsichords.

The compass of all but four of the instruments is C/E–c'''. (The Hieronymus Bononiensis now has a C/E–d''' keyboard and may originally have had a range of F–f''', lacking the low F♯ and G♯;[14] the Dominicus Pisaurensis has a C/E–f''' compass.) The lowest two chromatic keys of the Fenton House anonymous instrument are split, to provide the low F♯ and G♯; a unique feature of this keyboard is that the D and E keys (that is, the front portions of the F♯ and G♯ keys) cross over their neighbours, to the left, so that the D key raises the second jack and the E key, the third. (The front portion of the F♯ key crosses the F key, and the front portion of the G♯ key crosses the G key, the back portion of the F♯ key, and the F key.) The same split keys occur in the Boni harpsichord, which in addition has enharmonically divided keys for e♭/d♯, g♯/a♭, e♭'/d♯', g♯'/a♭', and e♭''/d♯''. In meantone temperament, this device enables a performer to play in the keys of E major, E minor, E♭ major, C minor, A♭ major, and F minor with the same purity of intonation as in the more usual keys. The Bristol anonymous has a keyboard of unusual interest because of the many divided keys, both accidentals and naturals. The arrangement of the bass notes suggested by Mr John Barnes on the basis of the order of the key levers is as follows:

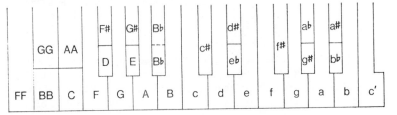

As indicated by the dashed line, the B♭ key is not actually divided but is merely scored so as to resemble its neighbours; the remaining e♭, g♯, and b♭ keys are, however, divided throughout, except for the highest octave, which has no divided keys.

The soundboards of most of the instruments listed are made of cypress, although that of the Nürnberg anonymous is pine and that of the Dominicus Pisaurensis is cedar, as is the whole of its inner case. This instrument possesses one especially interesting feature, to my knowledge unique in Italian harpsichords : between the bottom of the instrument and the soundboard there is an intermediate resonance board that lies exactly in the middle of the space between the bottom of the instrument and the soundboard; this resonance board is made of pine and appears to be of the same size as the soundboard.[15] Thus, it would seem to be similar to the counter-soundboards found in a few early Flemish and English instruments.[16] Another interesting feature of the Pisaurensis harpsichord is the very narrow wrestplank for the tuning pins, the nut being placed on a section of free soundboard between the wrestplank and the box slide. This construction also occurs in two non-Italian harpsichords of northern provenance, the claviorgan by the Fleming Lodewijk Theeuwes, made in London in 1579,[17] and a harpsichord by John Haward, in London in 1622.[18] One might be inclined to interpret the use of free soundboards in front of the jacks as an Italian feature, which was later introduced into Flanders and then into England. In any case, the dates of 1533 for the Italian instrument, 1579 for the Flemish example executed in England, and 1622 for the English example are suggestive. The wrestplanks of the Bertarinus and the Boni are massive blocks, while that of the Nürnberg anonymous was missing when, in 1962, the instrument became the property of the Museum. (It has been replaced in the style of that in the Dominicus Pisaurensis.)

The restoration of the Bertarinus harpsichord,[19] in the course of which a non-original second unison register was removed, thereby returning the instrument to its original single-strung disposition, presented an intriguing problem for which no solution was found until after the restoration was completed. Both of the jack slides had a disproportionately large distance between the two lowest slots (see figure 1). Furthermore, there was an extra hole in the front row of tuning-pin holes in the wrestplank. This front row must have been the original one, since scars left by an earlier nut partly overlap the second row of holes. (This original nut had been replaced by a new one when the second register was added.) There were considerable differences between the two jack slides, although both had the large distance between the two lowest slots. The narrower front slide with rather small slots was made of a

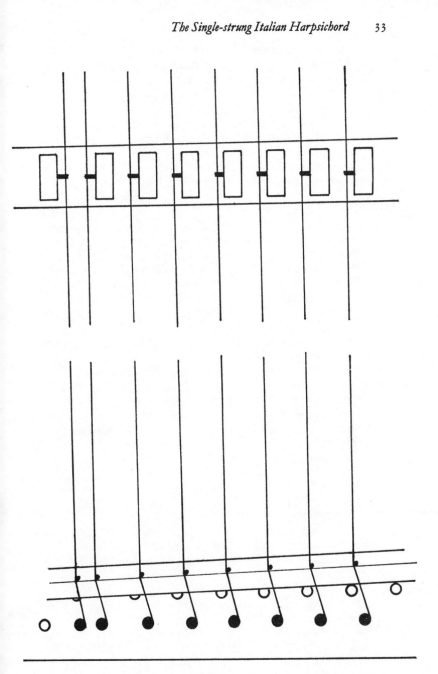

Figure 1

species of pine (*picea excelsa*) which, in Italy, grows only in the Alps. Therefore, it appeared doubtful that this slide originally formed part of an instrument that was most probably made in Rome. The material of the rear slide, which had larger slots and was of a much more substantial construction, was apple-wood which can be found throughout the Italian peninsula. The sides of this slide and the rear edge of the wrestplank had been planed down, obviously in order to allow the adding of the slide for the second register. Marks on the sides of the instrument clearly showed the original width of the wrestplank, which permitted determination of the original width of the rear slide. For the problem of the wide spacing between the two lowest slots, only the following solution presents itself : if the lowest jack had originally been turned round — that is, had plucked to the right while all the other jacks plucked to the left — the distance between the two lowest strings would have been smaller than that between any of the others, thus explaining the extra tuning-pin hole (see figure 2). In order not to bring the two lowest holes too close to each other, however, the distance between the two lowest jacks would have had to have been increased, thus explaining the wide spacing between the lowest two slots in the jack slides. Of course, when the second register was added, such a system involving two different directions of plucking in a single row of jacks had to be abandoned, and the spacing of the lowest tuning-pin holes found before the restoration became necessary. (The present writer is fully aware of the hypothetical character of this solution, since no such arrangement of the jacks has previously been observed in harpsichords, although it is found in virginals and spinets.)

The question of scaling is not difficult in the instruments mentioned here. The lengths of c″ fall between 262 mm (10.3) and 295 mm (11.6), clearly establishing that short-scaled Italian instruments, including examples with a C/E–f‴ range (the Dominicus Pisaurensis), existed in the sixteenth century. Hubbard[20] tends to assume stringing with gut rather than wire on single-strung harpsichords. The present writer is not inclined to concur in this view because of lack of convincing evidence and because of the beautiful tonal results of wire stringing on three of the instruments examined above. (In this connection, it should be noted that even Hubbard finds that the sound of an Italian harpsichord strung in gut is very poor.)[21]

The conclusions to be drawn from this group of instruments can be summarized as follows : Italian harpsichord-makers developed a comparatively standardized type no earlier than the seventeenth century. Before 1600, Italian makers produced several types that survived to a limited extent after 1600. Among these, one of the

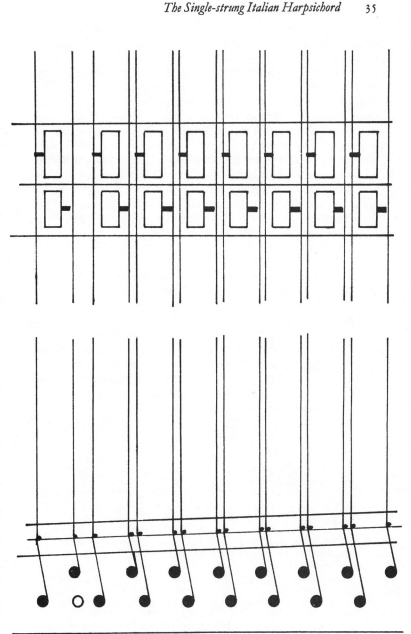

Figure 2

most interesting categories was the single-strung harpsichord, which was fairly common in the sixteenth century and which, even as late as Cristofori's time, had not become completely extinct. In addition, before the early seventeenth century, considerable variation of certain features in harpsichords can be found in Italian instruments. Cypress was not universally used as a material for the case; resonating surfaces were occasionally increased by a resonance board underneath the soundboard and by a small section of free soundboard under the nut; jacks with reversed plucking directions in the same register were occasionally used; and short scaling was used even on instruments with extended keyboard range. It is hoped that these conclusions will help to correct our views on the history of harpsichord-making in Italy, which still show a tendency to generalize from a standard type that developed only at a comparatively late date.

Acknowledgements

I wish to express my thanks to Professor Dr Richard Petzoldt of the Musical Instrument Museum of the Karl-Marx-Universität, Leipzig, for permitting me to examine the instruments by Dominicus Pisaurensis in that museum; to him and to Professor Ugo Procacci, Soprintendente alle Gallerie ed Opera d'arte delle Province di Firenze, Pistoia ed Arezzo, Florence, for their permission to publish photographs of instruments in their care; and, finally, to Dr J. H. van der Meer, Curator of the Musical Instrument Collections of the Germanisches Nationalmuseum, who took a lively interest in the completion of this article.

NOTES AND REFERENCES

1   A ninth example which came to my attention only as this article was going to press is in the Donaldson Collection at the Royal College of Music, London (no. 175). The instrument now has two unison registers and a keyboard range of C–d''', lacking the low C♯. According to Mr John Barnes of Edinburgh (to whom I am indebted for the information on this instrument), the harpsichord originally had only one register and probably had a C/E–f''' compass. It appears to have been built about 1580.

A single-strung harpsichord bearing the signature 'Giovanni Andrea Menegoni, 1690', in the Smithsonian Institution, Washington, D.C., is considered to be a nineteenth-century fake and therefore not discussed in this paper. See *A Checklist of Keyboard Instruments at the Smithsonian Institution* (Washington, D.C., 1967) no. 332,174. Also excluded is the *clavemusicum omnitonum*, built by Vitus de Trasuntinis in 1606 and preserved in the Museo Civico, Bologna. Its four octaves (C–c''') contain 31 keys each, giving a total of 125 keys. This instrument differs from those considered in this article in that the reasons for single stringing seem to have been purely practical; not only would there hardly be space for another two rows of tuning pins and another set of strings between the necessarily thin and delicate jacks, but also the problems of keeping even a single set of strings in tune must have bordered on the insuperable.

2 N. and F. Gallini *Museo degli strumenti musicali* (Milan 1963) no. 579

3 Museum no. 226–1879. F. Hubbard *Three Centuries of Harpsichord Making* (Cambridge, Mass., 1965) pp. 5, 8, 10, 14, 37; R. Russell *The Harpsichord and Clavichord* (London 1959) pp. 13, 27, 33, 34, plates 5, 6; R. Russell *Victoria and Albert Museum, Catalogue of Musical Instruments I, Keyboard Instruments* (London 1968) no. 1.

4 G. Kinsky *Musikhistorisches Museum von Wilhelm Heyer, Katalog, I* (Köln 1910) no. 67.

5 Museum no. 161. A list of the instruments preserved at the Museo Bardini is being prepared by the present writer.

6 Museum no. MIR 1071.

7 R. Russell *Catalogue of the Benton Fletcher Collection of Early Keyboard Instruments* (London 1957) p. 16.

8 R. Bragard and F. J. de Hen *Les Instruments de musique dans l'art et l'histoire* (Rhode-St-Genèse 1967) p. 104; V.-Ch. Mahillon *Catalogue descriptif et analytique du Musée Instrumental du Conservatoire Royal de Musique de Bruxelles III* (Ghent 1900) no. 1603.

9 I am indebted to Mr John Barnes for bringing this instrument to my attention.

10 A number of clavicitheria with only one stop exist most of which are of North European provenance—see T. Norlind *Systematik der Saiteninstrumente II, Geschichte des Klaviers* (Stockholm-Hannover 1939) col. 139. It is possible that single-strung harpsichords were also known in France, since Mersenne *Harmonie universelle* (Paris 1636) 'Liure Troisiesme, des Instrumens à Chordes', pp. 106, 110, explicitly speaks of 'double' and 'triple' harpsichords as having two and three sets of strings, respectively. Did he possibly know of a 'single' harpsichord having only one set of strings?

11 Norlind, op. cit., cols. 124, 125; C. Sachs *The History of Musical Instruments* (New York 1940) p. 340.

12 Leto Puliti 'Documenti estratti dall'archivio generale...,' *Atti dell'Accademia del Regio Istituto Musicale di Firenze* (Florence 1874) pp. 192, 196 (translated in part in Russell *The Harpsichord* p. 125). This inventory also lists another single-strung harpsichord without giving the maker's name.

13 F. J. Hirt *Meisterwerke des Klavierbaus* (Olten 1955) p. 134.

14 See Mr Barnes' article elsewhere in this volume.

15 I am indebted to Mr Jurisch, chief restorer of the Leipzig Museum, for drawing my attention to this matter; unfortunately, a closer examination was not possible, since there was only a small hole in the bottom through which the resonance board could be seen.

16 Hexagonal virginal by Joes Karest, Antwerp, 1548; rectangular virginals by Johannes Grauwels, Antwerp, c. 1580, and Adam Leversidge, London, 1666; harpsichords by John Haward, London, 1622, and Thomas Hitchcock, London, c. 1700. See Hubbard, op. cit., p. 48.

17 London, Victoria and Albert Museum, no. 125–1890; Russell *Victoria and Albert Museum Catalogue* no. 16.

18 Property of Lord Sackville, Knole Park, Sevenoaks, Kent. Russell *The Harpsichord* p. 66, plate 56.

19 The restoration was executed by Miss Olga Adelmann of the Staatliches Institut fur Musikforschung, Berlin, and the present writer in October, 1968. Publication of a detailed restoration report is planned.

20 Hubbard, op. cit., pp. 29 (footnote *a*), 327.

21 Ibid., p. 327 (footnote).

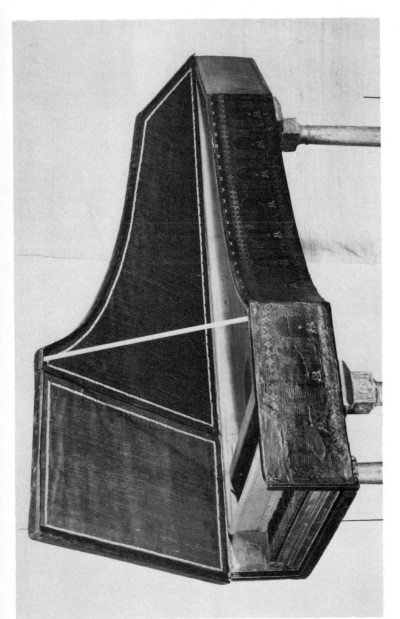

Single-strung Italian harpsichord, anon., 16th
century (Rück Collection, Germanisches Nationalmuseum, Nürnberg). *Friedemann Hellwig*

Detail of the ornamentation on the outer case of the
harpsichord shown in plate 35. *Friedemann Hellwig*

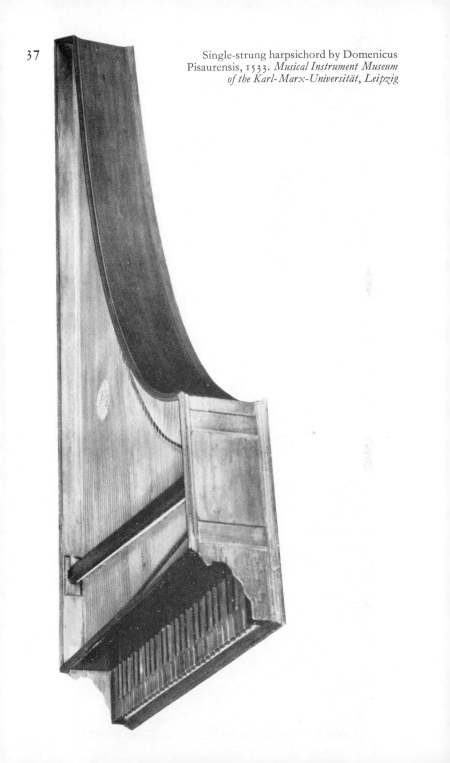

37

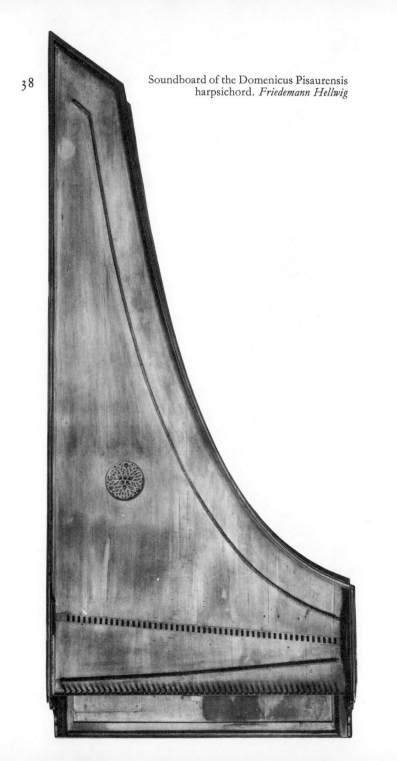

38

Soundboard of the Domenicus Pisaurensis
harpsichord. *Friedemann Hellwig*

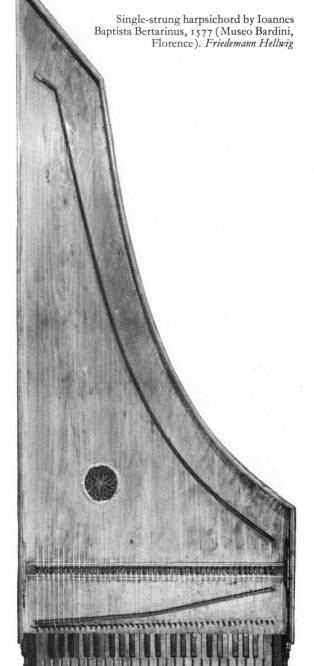

39   Single-strung harpsichord by Ioannes
Baptista Bertarinus, 1577 (Museo Bardini,
Florence). *Friedemann Hellwig*

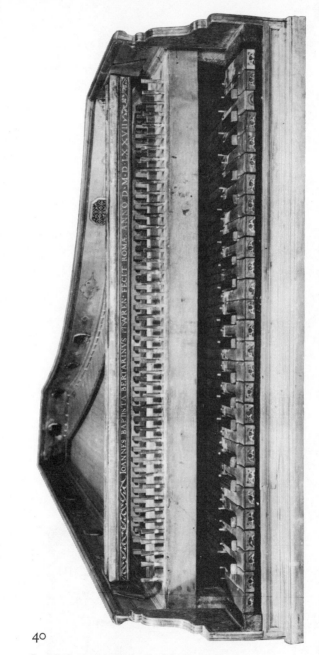

40

Inscription on the jackrail of the Bertarinus
harpsichord. *Friedemann Hellwig*

Documents dealing with the Ruckers Family and Antwerp Harpsichord-building

JEANNINE LAMBRECHTS-DOUILLEZ
Associate Curator, Museum Vleeshuis, Antwerp

Unearthing new documents dealing with the famous Ruckers workshop in Antwerp is a formidable task. Although hitherto unnoticed material must exist, it lies buried in widely scattered sources. Most of what is known about Antwerp harpsichord-builders comes from the membership lists of the Antwerp Guild of St Luke.[1] This work was supplemented in the publications of J. Denucé,[2] which are the principal source for the documents treated in this article.

Several of the inventories published by Denucé mention keyboard instruments, by far the richest being that of Jacques Snel (document I) which lists no less than six:

An organ with harpsichord with many registers, including a 'nightingale', the lid painted by Franchoys Borsse, the figures by Octavi Venus and the base by Snellincx.

A *steertstuck* harpsichord by Marten de Vos, the front board and the rear part of the lid by Daniel de Vos, his son.

An ordinary harpsichord by Ruckaert.

A double harpsichord by Ruckaert, leaf gilded, with a lid painting by Marten de Vos of the Prodigal Son.

Another double harpsichord by Ruckaert, [with a painting of] Orpheus by Franchoys Borsse [and other] figures by Roelken.

A small instrument, painted after Marten de Vos.

Ruckers instruments are also specifically identified in the inventories of Daniel Fourment (document II): 'A harpsichord by Jan Rucqueer with a base of hardwood'; and of Guill. Huymans (document III): 'A harpsichord, being a *steertstuck* by the elder Ruckers from the year 1588, which is placed in the organ loft of the Church of Carmelite Fathers, Brothers of the Blessed Virgin, to remain there so long as the present Father Superior shall remain in this city and no longer.'

However, as is shown by the items in document I, the instruments are more likely to be identified by the names of the painters who decorated them than by their builders. In his will of 1655 (document IV), Peter Muytincx 'desires that his daughter, Anna Catharina, shall keep the best harpsichord with base and painted cover by Jongen Franck', probably referring to Frans Francken the Younger (*c.*1581–1642). Other painters mentioned include Franchoys Borsse, whose name appears in Guild records between

1585 and 1620; 'Octavi Venus'—Otto van Veen (1597–1661); Daniel de Vos, listed in the Guild records in 1596; and Marten de Vos (c. 1531–1603), who painted the virginal lid showing Apollo and the Muses preserved in the Museum of Fine Arts, Brussels. The 'Snellincx' who decorated the claviorgan belonging to Jacques Snel (document 1) could have been any member of a family of Antwerp painters, Jan Snellinck (1544/1549–1638) or one of his sons, Daniel (1576–1627), Geraerd (1577–1669), Andreas (1587–1653), and Abraham (1597–1661). 'Roelken' remains as yet unidentified.

Painted harpsichord lids were already prized as separate works of art in the seventeenth century, as is shown by the inventory of Jan-Baptista Anthoine (document v), where a painted lid is separately valued at 100 florins.

Antwerp's importance as a centre of commerce is implied in an interesting pair of papers (document vi) dealing with 'five large spinets' belonging to Queen Christina of Sweden which were in Antwerp in May 1656 awaiting shipment 'by express to Rome'. On 8 June of the same year it is noted that the instruments had been shipped.

Also contained in the documents published by Denucé is a mention of 'a house called *Clavecimbel* [Harpsichord]' (document vii). Most houses of some importance had such names, usually illustrated in some decorative element in the façade, and the Vleeshuis Museum possesses sixteenth-century Antwerp majolica plaques for 'the Elephant' and 'the Pilgrim'. *Clavecimbale* appears to have been a popular name for houses in Antwerp. In the tax books for 1593–1605,[3] for example, three houses are listed with this name, the owners being Jan Heyndricx, Lambrecht van Kessel, and Symon de Bode. A house called *De clein clavesingel*—the small Harpsichord—on Jodenstraat was the property of the Ruckers family. It had originally been rented by Hans Ruckers the Elder at least as early as 1584[4] and was bought by him and his wife, Adriana Cnaeps, from Helena Shertoghe on 5 July 1597, with the proviso that the rent would continue to be paid until 15 March 1598.[5] In 1608 the house came into the sole possession of Hans Ruckers the Younger by the terms of an agreement made with his brother Andreas (document viii):

'Jodenstraet/North side/De clein clavesingel. The property of Hans Ruckers with surrender of heirship rights by Andries Ruckaerts by virtue hereof the last day of October 1608....Previously [held by] Hans Ruckaert under conveyance from Mistress Helena Shertoghe 5 July 1597....The act of the last day of October 1608 concerns a house with gate, large courtyard, pump, cistern, drains, store rooms, kitchen, business premises, land, and all appurtenances thereto situate and located in the Jodenstraet between the properties of Master Goossens Careest's house and the property to the east, and the warehouse and the property to the west, and also behind to the north, as that of the late Janne Rueckaerts their father and of their mother the same 5 July 1597 by conveyance obtained from Mistress Helena Shertoghe....'

As noted in document VIII, the house stood next to that of Goosen Karest, another harpsichord-builder, and by 1616 Andreas Ruckers was living not far away *bij Kerckhof, bij den scoenkramen* (now the Groenplaats en Schoenmarkt).[6] Clearly, the Antwerp harpsichord-builders lived close to one another, as did other groups of craftsmen in the sixteenth and seventeenth centuries.

The greatest importance of document VIII, however, is in the light that it casts on the long-disputed question of the date of Hans Ruckers' death. Most recent writers have concluded on the basis of the dates of instruments bearing the HR rose that the elder Ruckers lived until after 1620, accordingly assigning to him the series of payments to a Hans Ruckers for work on the organ of the St Jacob's Church between 1619 and 1623. Document VIII, on the other hand, establishes that Hans Ruckers the Elder was dead at least as early as 31 October 1608, although he was still alive on 5 July 1597. A recently discovered family tree dating from the eighteenth century[7] brings us nearer to the year suggested by Stellfeld and some earlier writers, namely 1598. This family tree shows 'descendants of Johannes Ruckers, who died in the century of 1500 in the years of 90';[8] thus, Hans Ruckers must have died between July 1597 and December 1599.[9]

DOCUMENTS

1. *1623, 21 January. Inventory of Jacques Snel, wine merchant living 'by Sint Jorispoorte' in Antwerp, who died on 17 January 1623*[10]
Een orgel met clavercimbel met veel registers, nachtegael ande andere, het scheel geschildert van Franchoys Borsse, de figuerkens van Octavi Venus ende den voet van Snellincx.
Een steertstuck clavecimbel van Marten de Vos, het vorste ende het achterscheel van Daniel de Vos zyn sone.
Een ordinaris clavecimbel van Ruckaert.
Een dobbel clavecimbel van Ruckaert, plat vergult, het scheel geschildert van Marten de Vos, van den Verloren sone.
Een ander dubbel clavecimbel van Ruckaert, eenen Orpheus van Franchoys Borsse, de personagien van Roelken.
Een cleyn instrumentken, geschildert nae Marten de Vos.

II. *1643, 23 July. Inventory of Daniel Fourment, living 'op doude Borsse',
who died on 5 June 1643*[11]
...Een Claversingel van Jan Rucqueer metten voet van herthout.

III. *1685, 6 October. Inventory of Guill. Huymans, living 'Meire
alhier'*[12]
...Spiegels ende schribaenen:
Een clavercinghel, wesende een steertstuck vanden ouden
Ruckaert, van het jaer 1588, delelcke alsnu berust op het oxael
inde kercke van Patres Carmeliten L.Vrouwenbroeders alhier,
om aldaer te blyven soo lange den tegenwoordigen Pater Sup-
prior binnen dese stadt sal blyven ende langer niet.

IV. *1655, 9 November. Will of Peter Muytincx, 'Oudt-Schepenen van
Antwerpen'*[13]
...Begeirende noch dat zijne dochter Anna Catharina sal
behouden de beste clavecimbale metten voet ende geschilderde
schelen van den Jongen Franck.

V. *1691. Inventory of Jan-Baptista Anthoine, 'riddere ende postmeester'.
living at 'Kipdorp', who died on 27 March 1687*[14]
...No 306. Een scheel van een Clavesingel f. 100.

VI. *1656, May. Inventory of goods belonging to Queen Christina of
Sweden 'pour envoyer à Rome, reposants en ceste ville d'Anvers...'*[15]
...Cincq epinettes grandes. Item, en une caisse appart, on
envoyera par exprès à Rome.
le huictiesme de juing 1656...Consetant ledict affirmant de ce que
dessus estre expedié ung ou plussieurs instruments in forma.

VII. *1666. Inventory of Geeraert van Dorth*[16]
Geeraert van Dorth, Coopman alhier...huyse genaempt Clavecimbel in de Rodestraete alhier.

VIII. *1608, 31 October. Agreement between Hans Ruckers the Younger
and Andreas Ruckers the Elder*[17]
Jodenstraet/Noordzijde/De clein clavesingel.
P[roprietaris] Hans Ruckers bij erffgevingen van Andries
Ruckaerts qua[litate] qua ult[im]o octobris 1608....Te vorens
hans Ryckaert bij transport van ju[fvrouw]e helena shertoghe
5 July 1597...Den brieff van ult[im]o octobris 1608 seyt een
huys met poorte, groote plaetse, pompe, regenback, weerdribbe,
neer camers, keuckene, comptoire, gronde en allen den toebe-
hoorten gestaan ende gelegen inde Jodenstr[aet] tusschen der
erffven M[eeste]r Goossens Careest huys ende erve oistwarts

ende goedshuys ende erve westwaerts ende oock achter noirt-
waerts gelyck dat verstorven is van wijlen Janne rueckaerts
hennen vader ende van henne moeder die ts[elve] 5 july 1597
bij transport gecregen hebben tegens Juf[vrouwe] helena
shertoghe....

NOTES AND REFERENCES

1　Published by Ph. Rombouts and Th. van Lerius *Les Liggeren et
autres archives historiques de la Gilde anversoise de Saint Luc*, 2 vols.
(Antwerp 1872; The Hague, n.d.; reprinted Amsterdam 1961).

2　J. Denucé *Bronnen voor de geschiedenis van de Vlaamse Kunst* : I, *Kun-
stuitvoer in de 17de eeuw te Antwerpen ; de firma Forchoudt* (Antwerp
1931); II, *De Antwerpsche 'Konstkamers' ; inventarissen van kunstver-
zamelingen te Antwerpen in de 16de en 17de eeuwen* (Antwerp 1932);
III, *Brieven en documenten betreffende Jan Brueghel I en II* (Antwerp
1934); IV, *Antwerpsche tapijtkunst en handel* (Antwerp 1936); V, *Na
Peter Pauwel Rubens ; documenten uit den kunsthandel te Antwerpen in de
17de eeuw van Matthys Musson* (Antwerp 1949).

3　Antwerp, City Archives, Privilegekamer, 2369, fols. 6, 52, and 87.

4　Antwerp, City Archives, Rekenkamer, 2227, fol. 17 verso, where
Ruckers' name appears as 'Hans Ruekers'.

5　Antwerp, City Archives, Schepenbrieven, 424, fols. 286–287.

6　J. A. Stellfeld *Bronnen tot de geschiedenis der Antwerpsche clavecimbel—en
orgelbouwers in de XVIde en XVIIde eeuwen* (Antwerp 1942) p. 94.

7　Reproduced in J. Lambrechts-Douillez *Antwerpse Klavecimbels in
het Museum Vleeshuis* [Antwerp] The Ruckers Genootschap [1970]
pp. 12–13.

8　'Descendenten van Joannes Ruckers gestorven/in den eeuwe 1500
in den jaren van 90'. See the present writer's 'Biographical notes
on the Ruckers-Couchet family' *Galpin Society Journal* XXII (1969)
98–9.

9　That Hans Ruckers the Elder is the subject of this reference is made
certain by the mention of Adriana Cnaeps as his wife.

10　Denucé, op. cit., II, pp. 35–9.

11　Ibid., II, p. 115; IV, p. 64.

12　Ibid., II, p. 333.

13　Ibid., p. 175.

14　Ibid., p. 364.

15　Ibid., pp. 176, 184, 186.

16　Ibid., p. 245.

17　Antwerp, City Archives, Privilegekamer, 2264, IX, fol. 309.

In Praise of Flemish Virginals of the Seventeenth Century

GUSTAV LEONHARDT
Harpsichordist, Amsterdam

In our time, aversion to the average, the common, and the popular is a feeling which some of us cannot help developing. Ear and eye, man's noblest senses, are confronted with such uniformities as endless rows of modern flats filled with loveless, standardized furniture, and with the non-stop wireless and tireless music heard in dwellings, shops, and even restaurants. These nourish the aversion and induce the unhappy few to attack the appalling normality with extravagant abnormality, to replace the common by the unheard-of, and to combat the unhealthy 'sanity' of the average with a cultivated madness.

Paradise seems to have got lost some 150 or 200 years ago, when the tastes of the educated and the uneducated started to diverge. Greatness and mediocrity, from differing only inconspicuously in the *how* but not in the *what*, gradually came to stand for the sublime and the trivial. Lord and servant formerly could have enjoyed the same galliard or minuet. Madame and the milkmaid could have joined in their admiration for the new façade of the castle. The simple merchant in the Netherlands could have ordered an instrument from the same well-known Ruckers workshop in Antwerp as did the Infanta of Spain. And many seventeenth-century ladies in the Low Countries—grand ladies, average ladies, common ladies, perhaps even popular ladies—liked the rectangular virginal. Moreover, they all liked to be depicted with their instruments, as is shown by the paintings of such Dutch masters as De Bray, van der Burgh, Codde, Dou, Duck, Duyster, Graat, D. Hals, de Hoogh, Kamper, Th. de Keyser, van Limborgh, van der Merck, Metsu, Molenaar, E. van der Neer, Netscher, Ochterveld, Palamedesz, van Velsen, van der Venne, Verkolje, Vermeer, Vinkeboons and de Witte.

Were they mistaken in liking the common? I think not. Things commonly liked and normally produced in those days did not speak against quality or taste, but for them.

Flemish and Dutch virginals—it seems impossible to make a distinction between the products of the southern and northern Netherlands, notwithstanding the fact that they were politically separated in the seventeenth century—were made in various sizes. After 1600, they all seem to have been rectangular in shape, with the keyboard recessed into the case and a four-octave compass (with a short octave in the bass). Of the larger-sized instruments, some had a plucking point close to the bridge and others almost at the middle of the string. Structurally, this was achieved by locating the keyboard either somewhat to the left or somewhat to the right of the middle of the front of the instrument. The pitch of these instruments varied; it may have been normal, a fifth higher,[1] or an octave above normal, the widths of the instruments being about 1,700 mm, 1,150–1,400 mm, and 810 mm (67, 45.5–55, and 32) respectively. The exterior was always painted, either plain or in different kinds of marbling. The interior (including the inside of the lid and the front panel) was either painted with gold bands or, more often, decorated with block-printed paper,[2] that on the lid being printed to resemble wood and generally serving as a background for a Latin motto. The different sections of this paper were set off by red and black bands. No part of the poplar wood of which the case was made was left visible. The soundboard had a rose with the maker's initials and was painted in tempera with flowers and birds, the borders being lined by an ornamental design. The natural keys were covered with bone; the accidentals were of wood, stained black. The bass strings were those nearest to the player, and the row of jacks cut the soundboard diagonally from the left front to the right rear. Two jacks facing in opposite directions were placed in each slot without any wooden separation between them (as would be the case in an Italian virginal).

Characteristic of the virginal is the fact that both nut and bridge —or should we call them both bridges?—are on the soundboard, contributing to the amplification of sound. The tuning pins are on the right. Scaling of the large type would be 340–350 mm (13.4–13.8) for c″; of the 'transposing' type, 240–290 mm (9.4–11.4); and of the octave instruments, about 170 mm (6.7). Most of the octave instruments may have been made as a part of a double virginal (the 'mother and child') giving 4¹ pitch coupled to the 8¹ pitch of the large instrument when placed on top of it.

The stand of the large or the 'transposing' instruments was invariably a separate unit that placed the virginal at a height which, to our eyes, is just between what would be comfortable for either a standing or a seated player. Most seventeenth-century paintings show the player standing, and this seems to be the preferable position, since the front lid-panel (which is hinged to the bottom of the case) interferes with the knees when the player is sitting. Perhaps the makers refrained from making the stand still higher for visual reasons.

The names given to virginals in the seventeenth-century Netherlands were, in general, *clavecimbel*, *vierkant*, and, in particular, *spinet*, for the 'left-keyboard' instrument and *muselar* for the 'right-keyboard' instrument. (The precise and penetrating tone of the *spinet* doubt-less inspired van Blankenburg[3] to give this name to the front 8^1 or 'lute' stop of his two-manual harpsichord.) These rectangular virginals were still found in many houses as late as the eighteenth century, but there is no evidence that they were still being made then. Rather, eighteenth-century builders had turned to the more graceful bentside spinets. In fact, judging mainly by what was happening in England, I believe that the disappearance of virginals during the last two decades of the seventeenth century, was primarily due to their appearance, by then considered sedate and clumsy.

The words of praise announced in the title of this article concern two very different kinds of sound, produced, respectively, by the nasal and precise *spinet* and the fluty and hollow *muselar*. This praise can, of course, only be evoked by instruments in the best condition. Extra barring on the soundboard or weak stringing, for instance, can easily spoil the tone. Both the *spinet* and *muselar* tone derive their beauty from the extremely sonorous burst of sound right after the attack. After this, the resonance quickly diminishes. Therefore, the beauty of *spinet* and *muselar* tone lies in its beginning rather than in sustaining power. Consequently, incorrect barring or weak stringing (I name only two of the most frequent faults), by sapping the initial sound, really spoil everything, leaving us somewhat bewildered and wondering how this dry, vague, and poorly sustained sound could ever have pleased anybody, let alone everybody.

The *spinet*, according to the number preserved and to seventeenth-century iconography, was less popular than the *muselar*, at any rate after 1620 or so. The *spinet* was closer in sound to the harpsichord of the day, and whereas this might have made it more popular, I suggest that a miniature harpsichord could not possibly have been what most people wanted if they chose the smaller one-register instrument. However this may be, the *spinet* has the attraction of a very even sound throughout the compass. No part dominates, and everything is crisp. Polyphonic music (if it is not slow) sounds well on it, as does music with a running bass or, for that matter, a running treble. Much of the keyboard music of the England of Elizabeth i to Charles ii goes well on it. It is not surprising, then, that in England only virginals of this 'left-keyboard' type were made. A statement as to which keyboard music of the Netherlands might have been conceived for the *spinet* seems hazardous and should even be considered impossible. Only the ear can judge which pieces come off well on a *spinet*, and I think it unlikely that a composer wrote specifically for one instrument rather than the other.

The *muselar* is more unusual in sound than the *spinet*. Some listeners hardly recognize it as belonging to the harpsichord family. The treble is rich and fluty, and (but for the short sustaining power) might be called 'singing'; it has, in fact, a declamatory quality of great strength. The tenor and bass registers are very full-sounding but have little definition, owing to the dominance of the fundamental tone. Thus, in the *muselar*, the treble and bass serve different functions, and homophonic music with a melodic treble part and a simple accompanying left-hand part (or parts) is especially delightful.

Many *muselars* had a special device for changing the tone of the lower half of the compass. This stop, the action of which corresponds to the well-known 'harp' or 'buff' stop (*lautenzug*) in harpsichords, brought small metal hooks into light contact with the vibrating strings close to the right-hand bridge. (This is the stop that Praetorius [4] calls the *arpichordum* and which, he says, gives a 'harffenirende Resonanz'.) The sound produced after the infuriating hours of adjustment required to make it even, is a delightful buzzing, which has the effect of even further separating the tone of the bass from that of the treble. Early pianofortes have a similar device (likewise for the lower part of the compass only) in the *fagottzug*, which employs a strip of parchment to create the buzz.

It cannot be denied that music with a quick bass causes difficulties on the *muselar*. The damping — effected at the point on the string at which the amplitude of vibration is largest — is noisy (van Blankenburg [5] compared the noise to the grunting of pigs). Furthermore, quick tone-repetition in the bass is unreliable. Nonetheless, judicious treatment is all a *muselar* needs. When treated well, its peculiar character is a continuous delight for the player, who soon forgets that his instrument has only one manual, only one stop, and only a four-octave compass.

NOTES AND REFERENCES

1   It seems likely that this pitch variation was analogous to that between the two manuals of transposing double harpsichords.
2   The design motifs for several of these papers were derived from *Variarum protactionum quas vulgo Marusias vocant libellus*, an ornament book by Balthasar Silvius printed in 1554.
3   Qu. van Blankenburg *Elementa musica* (The Hague 1739) p. 145.
4   M. Praetorius *Syntagma musicum* II (Wolfenbüttel 1619) p. 67.
5   Op. cit., p. 142.

More about Flemish Two-manual Harpsichords

JOHN HENRY VAN DER MEER
Oberkonservator, Germanisches Nationalmuseum, Nuremberg

Organology is one of the youngest branches of musicology, and one of the least developed. Until not so very long ago, musical instruments from former centuries were accepted at their face value, and iconographic as well as written documents concerning them were interpreted in a most uncritical fashion. This uncritical attitude was, among other things, detrimental to our knowledge of Flemish harpsichord-building in the sixteenth and seventeenth centuries; there are few surviving Flemish instruments from this period that were not changed in some way or other to suit the performance practice of a later time; thus, the uncritical attitude mentioned above renders certain works treating the subject nearly or completely worthless.[1]

Since World War II, however, the spirit of Anglo-American detective fiction has rapidly spread among organologists. Not only are the 'fingerprints' of the perpetrators of later alterations — many of them deleterious — placed under a magnifying glass, but attempts are also made to enter into the spirit — the 'psychology', as the writers of detective stories say — of the original makers. There is hardly a field in organology in which such detection is so widely practised as in that of two-manual Flemish harpsichords of the sixteenth and seventeenth centuries.

As Ripin[2] has pointed out, there are several categories of harpsichords that appear to be Flemish doubles. One group never saw any Antwerp harpsichord-maker's workshop whatsoever, but is made up, at the very best, of French instruments of the late seventeenth or eighteenth century (for example, the 1590 'Hans Ruckers' in private ownership in Brussels;[3] the 1590 'Hans Ruckers' in the Musée Instrumental du Conservatoire National de Musique, Paris, actually an instrument made in 1749 by Jean-Claude Goujon;[4] the 1636 'Joannes Ruckers' in Holyroodhouse, Edinburgh;[5] the 1617 'Andreas Ruckers' in the Neupert Collection in the Germanisches Nationalmuseum, Nürnberg;[6] the 1633 'Andreas Ruckers' in the Conservatorio di S. Pietro di Majella, Naples;[7] an undated 'Andreas Ruckers' in the Museum of Art at the Rhode Island School of Design, Providence, R.I.;[8] and an undated 'Andreas Ruckers' in private ownership in Brussels[9]). A second group consists of instruments built around original Flemish harpsichord or virginal soundboards (for example, the 1612 'Hans Ruckers', largely built by Pascal Taskin, now in the Musée Instrumental du Conservatoire Royal de Musique, Brussels;[10] the 1626 'Andreas Ruckers' in private ownership in Redhill, Surrey;[11] and the 1636 'Andreas Ruckers', again largely built by Pascal Taskin, in the possession of the Marchesa Olga di Cadaval, Colares, Portugal[12]). A third group consists of enlargements of Flemish one-manual harpsichords (for example, the 1639 Andreas Ruckers in the Gemeentemuseum, The Hague, now restored to its original one-manual state;[13] the 1651 Andreas Ruckers in the Victoria and Albert Museum, London;[14] the 1654 Andreas Ruckers in the Neupert collection in the Germanisches Nationalmuseum, Nürnberg;[15] the undated Joannes Couchet in the Metropolitan Museum of Art, New York;[16] and the 1669 Petrus Joannes Couchet in the Gemeentemuseum, The Hague[17]).

Now, if all these non-Flemish, largely non-Flemish, and altered Flemish doubles bearing the Ruckers and Couchet signatures are ruled out, only a small number of instruments remains. Virtually all of these appear to be built in a way that is unlike eighteenth-century doubles or to show signs of originally having been constructed in this fashion. Van Blankenburg and Verschuere Reynvaan[18]—a century and a century and a half, respectively, after the fact[19]—describe these remarkable Flemish doubles. It is little known that these writers put a flea into the ear of Hipkins,[20] who described these two-manual harpsichords as early as 1896. No consequences worth mentioning were, however, drawn from Hipkins' work until Sibyl Marcuse[21] described several surviving examples.

The instruments referred to are 'transposing' harpsichords, which have been discussed so frequently since Marcuse's brilliant article, that we can restrict ourselves to a short summary here. A transposer has an upper manual with a compass of $C/E-c'''$ and a lower manual with a compass of $C/E-f'''$, which is, however, 'shifted' in such a manner that the lower manual f''' jacks pluck the same strings as the upper manual c''' jacks, the lower manual thus transposing down a fourth with respect to the upper manual. Such an instrument possesses only two sets of strings—one 8^1 and one 4^1—and normally has four rows of jacks. Each manual operates one 8^1 and one 4^1 row, the two 8^1 rows plucking the same set of 8^1 strings, the two 4^1 rows the same 4^1 set.

The 1638 Joannes Ruckers in the Russell Collection at Edinburgh University[22] is such a transposing double in its original state, and the 1615 Andreas Ruckers in the Vleeshuis Museum, Antwerp,[23] was also clearly a transposer, the lower keyboard having, however, been refitted. A number of other instruments also show signs of having originally been transposers : the 1616

Hans Ruckers in private ownership in Paris;[24] an undated Hans
Ruckers in the Brussels Conservatoire;[25] possibly the 1618 Joannes
Ruckers in the Museum für Kunst und Kulturgeschichte, Dortmund;[26] the 1619 Joannes Ruckers double with a virginal in the
bentside in the Brussels Conservatoire;[27] the 1640 Joannes Ruckers
in Schloss Ahaus;[28] the 1642 Joannes Ruckers now in private
ownership in New York;[29] the 1637 Joannes Ruckers in the Museo
di Strumenti Musicali, Rome;[30] the 1608 Andreas Ruckers in the
Russell Collection;[31] the 1620 Andreas Ruckers in the Musical
Instrument Museum of the Staatliches Institut für Musikforschung,
Berlin;[32] the 1624 Andreas Ruckers in the Gruuthuuse Museum,
Bruges (now reduced to a single-manual instrument);[33] the 1633
Andreas Ruckers in the Musical Instrument Museum of the Karl-
Marx-Universität, Leipzig (also reduced to a single-manual instru-
ment);[34] and the 1646 Joannes Couchet in the Brussels Conserva-
toire.[35] Furthermore, in the Brussels Conservatoire's undated
Hans Ruckers (which now has both lute and 16¹ registers),[36] the
jack slide of the lute register originally came from a transposer and
the nuts still retain the small metal plates associated with the
duplicated E♭ strings of a typical transposer.

Now, van Blankenburg and Verschuere Reynvaan suggest that
all Flemish doubles until after 1630 were transposing instruments,
and there are contemporary documents which, if read superficially,
point to the same conclusion : the correspondence between the
painter Balthasar Gerbier and Sir Francis Windebank, private
secretary to King Charles I,[37] and a letter from the Paris court
organist Pierre de la Barre to Constantijn Huygens.[38] Hipkins did
indeed conclude that far into the seventeenth century all Flemish
doubles were transposers. This conclusion seems to be confirmed
by the fact that no surviving Flemish two-manual harpsichord
before 1642 can definitely be established originally to have been
non-transposing—'expressive' (as Hubbard puts it, not very hap-
pily) or 'contrasting' (according to the more appropriate termin-
ology of Ripin). The present author was once tempted to consider
the 1634 Joannes Ruckers in Ham House[39] as a nontransposer
because the instrument possesses only three jack slides, whereas
(according to the description of transposing doubles given by van
Blankenburg, Verschuere Reynvaan, and Hipkins) four slides
would have been necessary for a transposer. However, apart from
the fact that the Ham House Ruckers was rebuilt in England in the
eighteenth century, Ripin[40] has pointed out that the Flemish
makers must also have constructed three-slide transposing doubles.
Iconographic evidence (Jan Brueghel the Elder, 'Allegory of
Hearing' in the Prado Museum, Madrid) proves that three-slide
transposers, probably with C/E–c‴ on the upper and C/E–f‴ on

the lower keyboard, were built as early as *c.*1618. Therefore, the fact that a two-manual harpsichord contains only three rows of jacks is not sufficient evidence for supposing it originally to have been a contrasting double. Moreover, again on the basis of iconographic evidence (Jan Brueghel the Elder, 'Allegory of Hearing, Tasting, and Touching' in the Prado, as well as two family paintings by Cornelis de Vos, *c.*1622 and 1626, respectively), Ripin has shown that contrasting doubles were built by 1620 and demonstrated that the written documents referred to above can be interpreted in such a way as not to contradict this conclusion. The compasses of the instruments in question cannot be conclusively deduced from the paintings, the bass part of the keyboards not being shown. The instruments painted by de Vos may have a four-octave compass of C/E–c'''; the one in the Breughel picture reaches f''' in the treble and may have had a compass of C/E–f'''.

Although a contrasting double made by Hans Moermans the Younger in 1642 with a compass of GG–e''' exists in private ownership in Boston, Mass.,[41] no contrasting two-manual harpsichord with the compass of a normal one-manual Flemish instrument, C/E–c''' or occasionally C/E–d''' (for example, the 1637 Joannes Ruckers in the Russell Collection,[42] the 1651 Andreas Ruckers in Traquair House, Peebleshire,[43] or the undated Andreas Ruckers in the Vleeshuis Museum[44]) has hitherto been identified.

One instrument from the Ruckers workshops[45] is preserved, however, which in all probability was originally such a contrasting double with an upper keyboard duplicating the normal one-manual compass of C/E–c'''. This instrument (plate 41a, b) is in the Neupert Collection in the Germanisches Nationalmuseum at Nürnberg.[46] It has undergone several changes, very probably outside of Flanders in the late eighteenth century, and poses several problems. The first of these is that of the maker. There is an H R rose in the soundboard with a diameter of 85 mm (3.3), as is also found in the undated double 'Hans Ruckers' with lute and 16' registers in the Brussels Conservatoire[36] and in an undated single in private ownership in Ghent.[47] There is also a painted signature on the main jack rail : HANS RUCKERS ME FECIT ANTVERPIÆ ANNO 16.. (the two last figures illegible), which, however, is not executed in the normal Ruckers lettering and very probably dates from the eighteenth-century rebuilding. The date 1658 is painted on the soundboard near the rose, from which it follows that the instrument cannot have been built by Hans Ruckers, who died perhaps as early as 1598.[48] Several characteristics, however, make it highly probable that this harpsichord was indeed built in one of the Ruckers workshops, in which case the maker would have to have been Andreas the Younger. (The rose, if it is indeed genuine, would have to have been taken from another instrument.)

The case of the harpsichord has green garlands painted on a greyish ground in the style of the late eighteenth century, but there are traces of another painted decoration under the present one. Only x-ray examination will make it possible to decide whether the older decoration is indeed seventeenth-century Flemish. The interior of the lid carries the motto HÆC SI/ CONTINGANT MUNDO/ QUÆ GAUDIA CŒLI in gold letters on a blue ground. Probably the original printed paper on the lid—which in any case carried a different motto, as the present one is found exclusively in instruments actually made by Hans Ruckers—was damaged when the instrument was rebuilt in the eighteenth century. The stand is not original but is an addition of the nineteenth or early twentieth century. There are no endblocks for the keyboards.

The harpsichord now has a compass of C–c''' (with chromatic bass octave) in both manuals. The spruce keys, with bone naturals and stained oak accidentals, cannot possibly be Flemish for several reasons. The bone coverings of the naturals, although they have four grooves, do not have the typical Ruckers notches between the pairs of grooves; the key fronts have typical eighteenth-century mouldings; the D keys are wider than the other naturals, whereas typical Flemish keyboards have wide Bs, Cs, Es, and Fs; and the three-octave measure is only 485 mm (19.1) instead of the 500 mm (19.7) that is typical for Ruckers.

The keyframe of the lower manual is made of poplar with a balance rail of oak. The latter must date from the eighteenth century, as the whole of the keyframe probably does. The upper keyboard does not rest on a keyframe, but on a keyplank (plate 42), as is typical for Flemish upper manuals. This keyplank, since it must always have been part of an upper keyboard, makes it clear that the harpsichord must originally have had two manuals. This conclusion is confirmed by two measurements : although neither of the cheekpieces has been lengthened, the case is about 2 m (79) long and 275 mm (10.8) deep. Normal one-manual Flemish harpsichords have a length of about 1800 mm (71) and a depth of about 240 mm (9.4), for example, the following Joannes Ruckers harpsichords : 1627 in the Berlin Instrument Museum,[49] 1637 in the Russell Collection,[42] 1639 in the Victoria and Albert Museum,[50] and the following Andreas Ruckers instruments : 1618 in Berlin,[51] 1637 in the Rück Collection in the Germanisches Nationalmuseum,[52] 1640 in the Belle Skinner Collection at Yale University, New Haven, Conn.,[53] 1644 in the Vleeshuis Museum (Andreas the Elder),[54] 1648 recently acquired by the Musikhistorisk Museum, Copenhagen (Andreas the Younger),[55] and the undated example in the Vleeshuis Museum;[56] also, the two-manual 1654 Andreas Ruckers (originally a single) in the Neupert Collection.[15] Thus, the larger measurements of the two-manual 1658 Ruckers confirm that the instrument must have always had two manuals.

To return to the keyplank of the upper manual : it is made of poplar, but on both ends and at the back, strips of oak have been added. The oak strips at the ends can be explained by supposing that the keyplank was damaged in the process of removing the original endblocks, necessitating the addition of new wood. The oak balance rail is also a later addition. The original balance rail was placed somewhat nearer the front, as shown by the original balance-pin holes still visible in the plank. There are 45 of these, pointing to an original compass of C/E–c'''. The original three-octave measure revealed by these holes is 500 mm (19.7), as is to be expected in a Ruckers instrument. The original 45-note compass is confirmed by the following facts : between the two rows of 49 tuning pins for the 8' strings in the wrestplank there are 45 closed 8' tuning-pin holes (see plate 43); behind the 49 tuning pins for the 4' strings in the wrestplank there are 45 closed 4' tuning-pin holes; in the beechwood 4' bridge there are 45 closed pin holes; and in the soundboard there are 45 closed 4' hitchpin holes (plate 44). Both nuts and the 8' bridge, all of beech, are not original, nor is the wide gilt moulding in the style of eighteenth-century France or England that surrounds the soundboard and the wrestplank. The portion of this moulding inside the bentside functions as the 8' hitchpin rail, so that in this area there is no trace of a 45-note compass. However, the evidence of the upper-manual keyplank, the wrestplank, the 4' bridge, and the 4' hitchpins are sufficient to establish an undoubted 45-note compass of C/E–c''' in both manuals. The widening of the compass to C–c''' was made possible by replacing the original keys with slightly narrower ones and by taking away the endblocks of the keyboards.

The disposition poses some further problems. At present there are four rows of jacks : lute stop on the upper manual, dogleg 8' operated by both manuals, and 4' (all plucking to the bass), plus lower-manual 8' plucking to the treble in the back row; there are three rows of strings (8', 8', 4'). There is no trace of a buff batten. The lute stop can be declared non-original without any difficulty. It was added by sawing through the wrestplank diagonally and separating the parts, thus allowing space for an extra jack slide. The wrestplank (plate 45) is made of oak with a spruce covering, which, like the soundboard, is decorated with flowers painted in distemper. One of the flowers on the wrestplank comes dangerously near the slide for the dogleg jacks, so that it can be assumed that a slice was sawn off the back edge. Thus, it follows that the instrument in its original condition possessed only three slides and, since it was not a transposer, three rows of strings. Assuming this, one can very tentatively arrive at the conclusion that the original disposition was identical with that of the 1642 contrasting double of Hans Moermans the Younger,[41] the front register of which is a dogleg 8' operated by both manuals, with the lower-manual 8' in the middle row, and the 4' in the back row. One difficulty with this hypothesis is that only one row of closed 8' tuning-pin holes is visible in the wrestplank; for the moment it seems reasonable to assume that a second closed row lies under the very wide, non-original wrestplank moulding, although the final decision as to this point must be delayed until such time as the instrument is restored.

The present jack slides, each with 49 slots, are not original and probably date from the eighteenth-century alteration of the instrument. The jacks seem to be taken from a number of other harpsichords, as they are not homogeneous and the lower-manual 8' jacks are (for no reason) doglegged.

Considering the fact that a contrasting double from Moerman's workshop, dated 1642, is preserved, it need not surprise us that such an instrument was built in the Ruckers workshops in 1658. The Moermans is, however, progressive in having a GG–e''' compass, while the Ruckers with its C/E–c''' compass was extremely conservative. One can hardly imagine such an old-fashioned instrument being built after the middle of the seventeenth century by a Ruckers, if it was not the product of a tradition that had existed for several decades at least. The 1658 two-manual harpsichord in the Neupert Collection, together with the iconographic evidence already cited proves beyond doubt that the contrasting double was indeed one of the instruments produced in the workshops of the Ruckers family.

It is difficult to establish the precise original scaling for the 1658 contrasting double, since both the 8' nut and the 8' bridge are of later date. It is, however, possible to reconstruct the scaling approximately. In doing so, it appears that the 8' c'' must have had a vibrating string length of about 340 mm (13.4), which is the same as the vibrating length of the corresponding string in a C/E–c''' single harpsichord from the Ruckers workshop.[57] This confirms the assumption that, even if the HR rose cannot have originally belonged to the instrument, this harpsichord is indeed a product of that famous family of which organology is slowly detecting the secrets : the Ruckers of Antwerp.

NOTES AND REFERENCES

1   E.g. A. M. Pols *De Ruckers en de klavierbouw in Vlaanderen* (Antwerp 1942) and F. J. Hirt *Meisterwerke des Klavierbaus* (Olten 1955).

2   E. M. Ripin 'The two-manual harpsichord in Flanders before 1650' *Galpin Society Journal* XXI (1968) 33–9.

3   D. H. Boalch *Makers of the Harpsichord and Clavichord* (London 1956) Checklist of Ruckers Instruments, pp. 93–9, no. 3.

4   Boalch no. 4; G. Chouquet *Le musée du Conservatoire National de musique, Catalogue raisonné* (Paris 1875) no. 221; 2nd ed. (Paris 1884) no. 426; R. Russell *The Harpsichord and Clavichord* (London 1959) plates 21–3. I am indebted to Mme H. de Chambure for the information on the actual builder of this instrument.

5   Boalch no. 57.

6   Boalch no. 82; Inv. no. MINE 86; *Führer durch das musikhistorische Museum Neupert in Nürnberg* (n.p., n.d.) no. 50; H. Neupert *Vom Musikstab zum modernen Klavier*, 3rd ed. (Berlin 1952) p. 20; H. Neupert *Das Cembalo*, 2nd ed. (Kassel-Basel 1951) p. 38; Pols, op. cit., plate 7.

7   Boalch no. 101; J. H. van der Meer 'Flämische Cembali in italienischem Besitz' *Studien zur italienisch-deutschen Musikgeschichte* III (1966) 114–21.

8   Boalch no. 131.

9   Boalch no. 134; J. H. van der Meer 'Ruckers' *Die Musik in Geschichte und Gegenwart* XI, plate 58.

10   Boalch no. 17; S. Marcuse *Musical Instruments at Yale. A Selection of Western Instruments from the 15th to 20th Centuries, Catalogue* (Yale University Art Gallery 1960) p. 8; F. Hubbard *Three Centuries of Harpsichord Making* (Cambridge, Mass., 1965) p. 54.

11   Boalch no. 95.

12   Boalch no. 104.

13   Boalch no. 105; J. H. van der Meer 'An example of harpsichord restoration' *Galpin Society Journal* XVII (1964) 5–16.

14   Boalch no. 118; P. James *Early Keyboard Instruments From Their Beginnings to the Year 1820* (London 1930) plate XLII; Pols, op. cit., plate II; Gh. Juramie *Histoire du piano* (Paris 1948) p. 40; Hirt, op. cit., pp. 14–15; R. Russell *Victoria and Albert Museum, Catalogue of Musical Instruments I, Keyboard Instruments* (London 1968) no. 14.

15   Boalch no. 119; Inv. no. MINE 85; *Führer* no. 133.

16   *The Metropolitan Museum of Art, Catalogue of the Crosby Brown Collection of Musical Instruments of All Nations, I, Europe* (New York 1904) no. 2363; E. M. Ripin 'The Couchet harpsichord in the Crosby Brown Collection' *Metropolitan Museum Journal* II (1969) 169–78.

17   Pols, op. cit., plate 13; Ripin 'The Couchet Harpsichord' fig. 6.

18   Qu. van Blankenburg *Elementa musica* (The Hague 1739) pp. 142–5; J. Verschuere Reynvaan *Muzykaal kunstwoordenboek* (Amsterdam 1795) pp. 112–13.

19   Hubbard, op. cit., p. 72.

20   A. J. Hipkins *A Description and History of the Pianoforte and of the Older Keyboard Stringed Instruments* (London-New York 1896) pp. 81–90.

21   S. Marcuse 'Transposing Keyboards in Extant Flemish Harpsichords' *Musical Quarterly* XXXVIII (1952) 414–25.

22   Boalch no. 61; Russell *The Harpsichord* plates 33–5; *The Russell*

Collection and Other Early Keyboard Instruments in Saint Cecilia's Hall,
Edinburgh (Edinburgh 1968) no. 6.

23   Boalch no. 79; *Catalogus Oudheidkundige Musea Stad Antwerpen,*
Vleeshuis v, *Muziekinstrumenten* (Deurne–Antwerpen, n.d.) no. 33.

24   Boalch no. 22; Russell *The Harpsichord* p. 45 and plate 36.

25   Boalch no. 26; V.-Ch. Mahillon *Catalogue descriptif et analytique du*
Musée Instrumental du Conservatoire Royal de Musique de Bruxelles,
5 vols (Ghent-Brussels 1893–1922) no. 2934; Russell *The Harpsi-*
chord p. 45.

26   Boalch no. 35. I am indebted to Dr Horst Appuhn for allowing
me to study this instrument. The Dortmund museum has not yet
been rebuilt since being damaged in World War II, and its objects
are partly exhibited and partly in storage in Schloss Cappenberg.
Owing to the crowded storage conditions, I was not able to make a
complete examination of this instrument.

27   Boalch no. 37; Mahillon, op. cit., no. 2935; James, op. cit., plate
XXXVII; Pols, op. cit., plate 10; Hirt, op. cit., pp. 290–1; P. Col-
laer and A. Vander Linden *Historische atlas van de muziek* (Amster-
dam-Brussels 1961) illus. 261; cf. Russell *The Harpsichord* pp. 45,
149.

28   Boalch no. 63; Rudolf Reuter 'Das Ruckers-Cembalo der Grafen
von Landsberg-Velen' *Westfalen* XLVI (1968) 123–8.

29   Boalch no. 64; *Illustrated Catalogue of the Music Loan Exhibition, held*
...June and July 1904 (London 1909) p. 170; see also *Musical Times*
XLV (1904) 431.

30   Boalch no. 71; Van der Meer 'Flamische Cembali'.

31   Boalch no. 72; *The Russell Collection* no. 3; Russell *The Harpsichord*
plate 38.

32   Boalch no. 84; C. Sachs *Sammlung alter Musikinstrumente bei der*
Staatlichen Hochschule für Musik in Berlin, Beschreibender Katalog (Berlin 1922) no. 2230; A. Berner 'Zum Klavierbau im 17. und 18.
Jahrhundert' *Kongress-Bericht Gesellschaft für Musikforschung, Lüne-*
burg 1950 pp. 239–43.

33   Boalch no. 92.

34   Boalch no. 100; G. Kinsky *Musikhistorisches Museum von Wilhelm*
Heyer in Cöln, Katalog I (Cologne 1910) no. 71; H. Ruth-Sommer
Alte Musikinstrumente (Berlin 1916) pp. 69, 90.

35   Mahillon, op. cit., no. 276.

36   Boalch no. 25; Mahillon, op. cit., no. 2510.

37   W. N. Sainsbury *Original Unpublished Papers Illustrative of the Life of*
Sir Peter Paul Rubens (London 1859) pp. 208–10; Russell *The*
Harpsichord pp. 161–2; Hubbard, op. cit., pp. 231–2.

38   W. J. A. Jonckbloet and J. P. N. Land *Musique et Musiciens au XVII*e
siècle (Leyden 1882) p. CXLIX

39   Boalch no. 54; Russell *Victoria and Albert Museum Catalogue* no. 12.

40   Ripin 'The two-manual harpsichord'.

41   Information supplied by the owner, Mr William Post Ross.

42   Boalch no. 59; *The Russell Collection* no. 5; Boalch *Makers* plate VII.

43   I am indebted to Messrs J. J. K. Rhodes and W. R. Thomas, Burn-
tisland, Fife, for showing me the Traquair House Ruckers, which
they have restored.

44   Boalch no. 130; *Catalogus* no. 35.

45   I am here excluding the two-manual 1681 Joris Britsen, originally
in the Régibo Collection, with a compass of four octaves and a note,
as being too late.

46   Boalch no. 24; Inv. no. MINE 84; *Führer* no. 45; *Führer durch die Ausstellung historischer Musikinstrumente und graphischer Musikdarstellungen in Bamberg, Neue Residenz, 15. Juli mit 16. August 1953 aus Anlass des internationalen musikwissenschaftlichen Kongresses der Gesellschaft der Musikforschung* (n.p., n.d.) no. 15.

47   Boalch no. 29.

48   See Dr Lambrechts-Douillez' article elsewhere in this volume.

49   Boalch no. 43; Sachs, op. cit., no. 2227; E. van der Straeten *La musique aux Pays-Bas avant le 19e siècle* III (Brussels 1875) pp. 330–2; Pols, op. cit., plate v.

50   Boalch no. 62; Russell *Victoria and Albert Museum Catalogue* no. 13.

51   Boalch no. 83; Sachs, op. cit., no. 2224.

52   Boalch no. 106; Inv. no. MIR 1073; van der Meer 'Ruckers' *Die Musik in Geschichte und Gegenwart* XI plate 57.

53   Boalch no. 109; W. Skinner *The Belle Skinner Collection of Old Musical Instruments* (Holyoke, Mass., 1933) no. 20; Hirt, op. cit., pp. 12–13.

54   Boalch no. 112; *Catalogus* no. 34; *Algemene Muziekencyclopedie* IV (Antwerp 1960) frontispiece.

55   Boalch no. 117.

56   Boalch no. 130; *Catalogus* no. 35.

57   Hubbard, op. cit., p. 58.

41 a

lans Ruckers' harpsichord of 1658 (Neupert
ollection, Germanisches Nationalmuseum,
ürnberg). *Friedemann Hellwig*

41 b

Top view of the Ruckers
harpsichord. *Friedemann Hellwig*

Upper-manual keyplank of the Ruckers harpsichord
Friedemann Hellwig

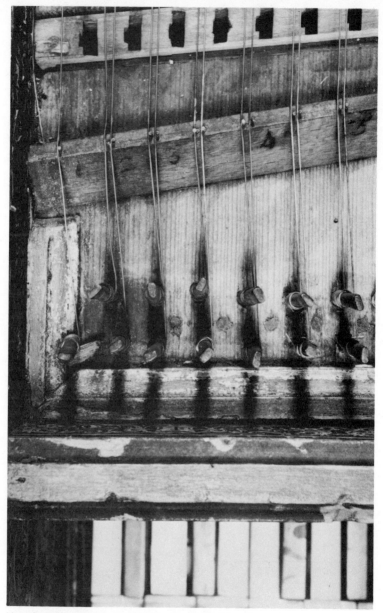

43

Detail of the wrestplank of the Ruckers harpsichord
showing plugged tuning-pin holes.
Friedemann Hellwig

44

Detail of the soundboard of the Ruckers harpsichord, showing plugged 4′ hitchpin holes.
Friedemann Hellwig

Wrestplank of the Ruckers harpsichord.
Friedemann Hellwig

The Tabel Harpsichord

CHARLES MOULD
Administrator, Oxford Polytechnic

In the study of the English harpsichord, it is almost inevitable that the subject of the Tabel harpsichord should be raised, since in the past it was customary to regard this instrument as the direct antecedent of the Kirckmans and Shudis of the later eighteenth century. However, before examining the Tabel harpsichord itself, it is useful to examine the relationship between Tabel, Shudi, and Kirckman. Burkat Shudi and Jacob Kirckman were both of North European extraction, Shudi having come from Glarus in Switzerland to settle in England in 1718 and Kirckman having come from Bischweiler near Strasbourg in the early 1730s. The style of their instruments owes much to the Flemish school of harpsichord-building, and this similarity is usually attributed to the fact that both men were at one time the apprentices of Hermann Tabel.

Tabel came from the Low Countries, and James Shudi Broadwood writing in 1838 related that Tabel learned his business in the shop of 'the successors of the Ruckers at Antwerp'.[1] It is not possible to establish when Tabel was born, but the earliest records of his trade in London date from 1716, by which time he must have completed his apprenticeship in Antwerp. He must therefore have been at least twenty-five years of age in 1716, and he was probably ten years older. The successors to the Ruckers were the Couchets, and the latest dates ascertained for any members of the family are in the 1680s. Accordingly, it would seem quite likely that Tabel was well into middle age in 1716, when he set up in Oxenden Street in London, and that he was actually born in the 1660s.

In 1723 Tabel was moved to place the following announcement in the *Evening Post* of 30 May:

'Mr Tabel, the famous harpsichord maker, has three harpsichords to dispose of, which are and will be the last of his making, since he intends to leave off business. At his house in Oxenden Street over against the Black Horse in Piccadilly.'

A year later, Tabel moved to Swallow Street, where he remained until his death.

Despite the apparent finality of this notice, Tabel inserted a further notice in the *St. James' Evening Post* of 22–24 February 1733:

'Whereas it has been reported, that Mr TABEL, the famous Musical Instrument maker, was dead, and that he hath learn'd

his Art to one of his Men, to make that fine Tone in Harpsichords, all which is false and foundless, he lives still at his House
in Swallow-street, over-against Haddon-Court, near Golden
Square.'

It would appear that during the ten years separating these an-
nouncements, both Shudi and Kirckman had worked in his shop,
and it was perhaps the support of those able men which determined him to continue in work long after he had intended to
retire. By 1729, Shudi must have broken away, for his first instrument is dated in that year, but Kirckman remained and was
nominated by Tabel as one of his trustees. In his will of 1738, Tabel
bequeathed £5 to Kirckman for mourning. Either Kirckman took
his duties as a trustee very seriously, or he was a very shrewd
business-man—his subsequent wealth suggests the latter—for he
married Tabel's widow almost immediately after Tabel's death. It
is amusing to read Burney's description, in Rees' *Cyclopaedia*, of the
way in which Kirckman carried out his courtship.

'Kirchmann worked with the celebrated Tabel as his foreman and
finisher till the time of his death. Soon after which, by a curious
kind of courtship, Kirchmann married his master's widow, by
which prudent measure he became possessed of all Tabel's
seasoned wood, tools and stock-in-trade. Kirchmann himself
used to relate the singular manner in which he gained the widow,
which was not by a regular siege but by storm. He told her one
fine morning at breakfast that he was determined to be married
that day before twelve o'clock. Mrs Tabel in great surprise,
asked him to whom he was going to be married, and why so
soon? The finisher told her that he had not yet determined whom
he should marry, and that if she would have him he would give
her the preference. The lady wondered at his precipitancy, hesi-
tated full half an hour, but he continuing to swear that the business must be done before twelve o'clock that day, at length she
surrendered; and as this abridged courtship preceded the marriage act, and the nuptials could be performed at the Fleet or
May Fair without loss of time or hindrance to business, the
canonical hour was saved, and two fond hearts were in one
united in the most summary way possible just one month after
the decease of Tabel.'

Unfortunately, the marriage did not last long, for Susanna (who
had held the three surnames of Virgoe, Tabel and Kirckman) died
in 1740. By 1739, Kirckman had moved to his own premises, where
he was to remain for at least ten years. That he took all of his late
master's stock with him is made clear by the following notice in the
Daily Gazetteer of 8 May 1739:

'Whereas Mr Hermann Tabel late of Swallow Street, the famous

Harpsichord maker, dead, hath left several fine harpsichords to be disposed of by Mr Kirckmann, his late Foreman; this is to acquaint the Curious that the said Harpsichords, which are the finest he ever made, are to be seen at the said Mr Kirckmann's, the corner of Pulteney Court in Cambridge Street, over against Silver Street, near Golden Square.'

The one instrument which is left to us from the workshop of Tabel has been the subject of much discussion. In the past ten years or so, it has become the custom to decry it. Hubbard[2] has stated that it is 'of dubious origin', and R. Russell[3] wrote that 'there is no original feature to suggest the work of Tabel in particular'. Boalch[4] cites the many changes in its life and ownership and goes on to say that 'the general style suggests that it was made a great deal later than its nameboard suggests'. In the light of all this controversy, it seems pertinent to sift the evidence, and to make a close study of the instrument. The following account of the instrument was made after a detailed examination had been carried out at the County Museum, Warwick. The instrument was acquired by the Museum on 2 July 1965, and the writer is indebted to the Curator, Miss Jocelyn M. Morris BA, FSA, FMA, for her help in the examination.

The Tabel harpsichord resembles a Kirckman instrument in shape, finish and scale (plates 46 and 47). The case is of walnut, cross-banded, but without stringing. The banding is less elaborate than that found on later instruments, in that the longitudinal bands are carried to the outer edges of the case panels without mitreing into the vertical bands. These vertical bands are thus of the same height as the panels which they surround. The bentside has only one curve, as in almost all English eighteenth-century instruments. The lid is held by strap hinges, which are identical to those of the Thomas Hitchcock harpsichord belonging to the Victoria and Albert Museum, London. It seems likely that fittings for harpsichords were made by specialists in this work rather than by individual makers, as is still the case today, and if we accept the fact that the Hitchcock is dated somewhere in the first quarter of the eighteenth century, this adds weight to the argument that the Tabel is of a similar period. These hinges are not found with the same markings on any other English instrument, with the possible exception of an instrument by William Smith which has recently been found in Oxford. This latter instrument appears to be of the same date as the Hitchcock, and the small hinges on the boards over the keys and action are of a design very similar to those on the Tabel.

The Tabel harpsichord has no pedals, swell, machine, or music desk, the existence of any one of which would point to a date later than 1721, the date appearing on the nameboard. The instrument stands on a simple turned trestle stand, which could well be original. The external dimensions of the instrument are : length, 2470 mm (97¼); width, 943 mm (37⅜); and depth of case including the lid, 286 mm (11¼). The case thickness varies between 18 and 19 mm (¹¹⁄₁₆ and ¾); the bottom boards of the case run transversely under the keys and action, longitudinally under the soundboard. This is standard eighteenth-century practice, but in instruments of earlier date the bottom boards run longitudinally throughout, except for a narrow strip at the keyboard end.

The main interior veneer is sycamore. This is inlaid with double quarter-inch stringing of light walnut, which runs the length of the board above the keys, out onto the key surrounds, and then downward through a right angle to disappear behind the lower-manual endblocks. The nameboard bears the inscription HERMANUS TABEL ' FECIT LONDINI J7ZI, executed in black paint (plate 48). The style of this inscription looks backward to the inscriptions on the Ruckers instruments, and is much the same as that on the nameboard of the earliest surviving Shudi harpsichord, which is dated 1729.

The keyboards of the instrument present a strange and interesting problem. The external finish of the naturals is ebony, and the accidentals are of pine, topped with ivory slips. Boalch states that in 1900 Broadwoods (the successors to the firm created by Shudi) restored the instrument, and this is borne out by an ink-written paper slip which is pasted above the right-hand side of the wrestplank: 'Double Harpsichord by Tabel restored by John Broadwood and sons May 1900. Tune semitone below French.' Boalch goes on to say that in this restoration the naturals were refaced, and their present excellent condition suggests that the present keytops are the result of this restoration. The keys themselves are undoubtedly original. The compass is five octaves from FF–f‴ with no bottom FF♯, a compass which is standard English harpsichord practice even today. The keys are of pine, in places somewhat crudely finished, and their authenticity (indeed, that of the whole instrument) seems to be established by an ink inscription in longhand on the top key of the lower manual : 'No 43 Herm Tabel Fecit Londini 1721' (plate 49). This inscription seems to have been overlooked by all other writers describing the harpsichord, although it is readily visible on withdrawing the upper manual. The key balance is interesting, since it differs on the two manuals. The upper manual has an apparently original balance rail and all the keys, both accidentals and naturals, are balanced along the same line. In order to compensate for the fact that with this system the touch of the accidentals would be heavier than that of the naturals, the latter all have a transverse weight at the distal end. The keys are prevented from lateral movement by thin pins between them at the distal end. This system is occasionally found on English spinets, and a similar arrangement is to be seen on the lower manual of the Hitchcock. The lower-manual keys have a similar row of balance holes, and matching holes in the keybed show that at one time the keys were balanced at this point. At some later date, however, a new balance rail was substituted for the original, and new mortises were cut so that the naturals are balanced 12 mm ($\frac{1}{2}$) further and the accidentals 28 mm ($1\frac{1}{8}$) further toward the distal end of the key. Thus, the lower manual is now balanced in the traditional staggered way. The keys are equipped with front pins to prevent lateral movement. It is tempting to surmise that this change to the lower manual was carried out by Broadwoods, but the style of the staggered balance mortises is so like the original 'in-line' mortises that they look as if they were all cut at the same time, or at least by the same workman. Is it possible that Tabel did this himself? Regardless of who may have made the change, it is difficult to understand why only one manual was altered.

The instrument has a conventional English disposition of 8^1 dogleg for the upper and lower manuals, lute on upper, and second 8^1 and 4^1 on the lower manual. This is the same as is found on many other instruments after the Tabel. There is also no element of this disposition which is not found elsewhere on earlier English harpsichords, and it is difficult to assume that it was the influence of Tabel alone which caused Shudi and Kirckman to adopt similar specifications for their standard two-manual instruments. There are no harps, and the registers are operated by curious 'bobbin'-shaped stop knobs. There are, in fact, two different styles of bobbin—one short and fat, one long and thin—and there is one of each on either side of the instrument. The stop levers are rather crudely made and are gilded. The jacks and slides are modern but made in an authentic eighteenth-century style.

The soundboard grain is laid longitudinally and, where the thickness can be measured near the jack slide, it appears to be approximately 3 mm ($\frac{1}{8}$) thick. It is to be hoped that in a subsequent restoration it will be possible to measure the whole of the soundboard, and to record the style of the barring and the inner case construction. At present, dowels and nail heads on spine and bottom boards indicate that the internal bracing must be similar to that found on Kirckman and Shudi instruments.

Boalch in his description states that the 4^1 bridge was moved by Broadwoods. That the bridge was moved is quite obvious, since a tell-tale scar and nail holes distal to the present bridge reveal its original position. It seems quite likely that the 8^1 bridge was moved as well, despite the fact that a thin strip of beech glued to the soundboard just distal to the 8ˈ bridge covers the area that would have been scarred if the bridge had been removed. The 4ˈ scaling as deduced from the scars on the soundboard implies a longer 8ˈ scale than the present 342 mm ($13\frac{1}{2}$), which is about average for eighteenth-century instruments the size of the Tabel. If this reasoning is correct and if the 8ˈ bridge originally occupied the area covered by the beech strip, the 8ˈ scaling was originally about 362 mm ($14\frac{1}{4}$), which would have been long by mid-eighteenth-century standards. Thus, the bridges may have been moved at an earlier date than Broadwoods' restoration.

The authenticity of the instrument is further supported by comparison of the signature on the key with Tabel's signature on his will at Somerset House, London. The two are so similar as to leave little doubt that Tabel himself signed the instrument. In addition, the soundboard of the instrument contains a rose (plate 50) made up of intertwined initials that is similar in design to some Kirckman roses of later date and to the rose in an instrument made by J.D.Dulcken in 1745. In the Tabel harpsichord, the initials are surmounted by a viscount's coronet, and it was formerly supposed that the initials were those of the instrument's original titled owner. The true origin of the design is, however, immediately apparent from Tabel's will, since the self-same cipher appears next to his signature as his seal (plates 51 and 52).

The nuts and bridges are all of conventional eighteenth-century pattern, and their only unusual feature is that they do not taper from bass to treble as markedly as in later instruments. Before leaving the constructional details, it should be mentioned that the spine is of oak, and this appears to be the earliest English harpsichord in which pine was not used for the spine.

In conclusion, it is fair to say that, as has been observed by earlier writers, in most respects the Tabel harpsichord does not differ significantly from the instruments of Kirckman and Shudi. The fact that both men were apprenticed to Tabel gives considerable weight to the argument that this instrument is the direct antecedent of the later English harpsichords. If this is indeed the case, Tabel's influence is detectable only in the long scaling, which is more consistent with Flemish practice than with English practice in the early eighteenth century. The principal aspect of the problem which has now received some strengthening is the question of the instrument's authenticity. It would seem that the inscription on the keys, together with the style of the hinges, must point to the correctness of the date and to the hitherto unrecorded fact that by 1721 Tabel had made at least 43 instruments, unless he cheated by not numbering them consecutively. Although this is not a large output, it seems almost unfair that no other instrument has survived. It is to be hoped that, with the resurgence of interest in the harpsichord, more instruments by Tabel will come to light and be available for detailed examination.

Present Scaling of the 1721 Tabel Harpsichord

Note	Longer 8' string length		Plucking point (front 8')		Plucking point (lutè)		4' string length	
	mm	inches	mm	inches	mm	inches	mm	inches
f'''	127	5	57	$2\frac{1}{4}$	13	$\frac{1}{2}$	54	$2\frac{1}{8}$
f''	254	10	73	$2\frac{7}{8}$	16	$\frac{5}{8}$	114	$4\frac{1}{2}$
c''	343	$13\frac{1}{2}$	79	$3\frac{1}{8}$	19	$\frac{3}{4}$	151	$5\frac{15}{16}$
f'	533	21	92	$3\frac{5}{8}$	22	$\frac{7}{8}$	248	$9\frac{3}{4}$
f	991	39	118	$4\frac{5}{8}$	32	$1\frac{1}{4}$	476	$18\frac{3}{4}$
F	1499	59	143	$5\frac{5}{8}$	44	$1\frac{3}{4}$	788	31
FF	1841	$72\frac{1}{2}$	168	$6\frac{5}{8}$	57	$2\frac{1}{4}$	1048	$41\frac{1}{4}$

NOTES AND REFERENCES

1   *Some Notes Made by J. S. Broadwood, 1838, with Observations and Eluci-dations by H. F. Broadwood, 1862* (London 1862) p. 4.
2   F. Hubbard *Three Centuries of Harpsichord Making* (Cambridge, Mass., 1965) p. 158.
3   R. Russell *The Harpsichord and Clavichord* (London 1959) p. 79.
4   D. H. Boalch *Makers of the Harpsichord and Clavichord* (London 1956) p. 122.

46

Front view of the Tabel harpsichord (County Museum, Warwick). *Charles Mould*

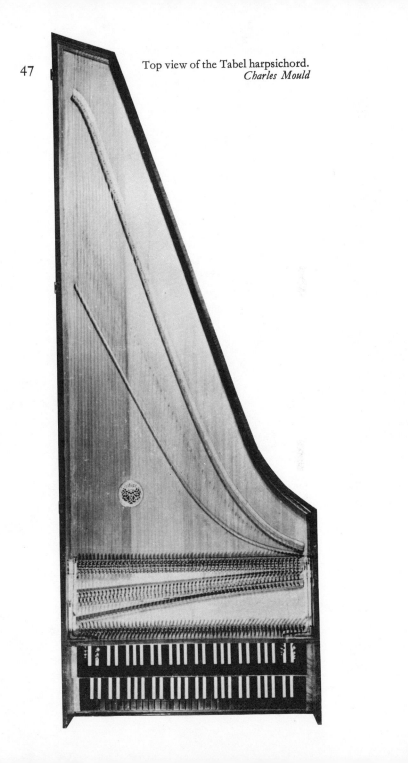

Top view of the Tabel harpsichord.
Charles Mould

Nameboard of the Tabel harpsichord. *Charles Mould*

49   Tabel's signature on the top key of the lower manual. *Charles Mould*

50

Rose of the Tabel harpsichord. *Charles Mould*

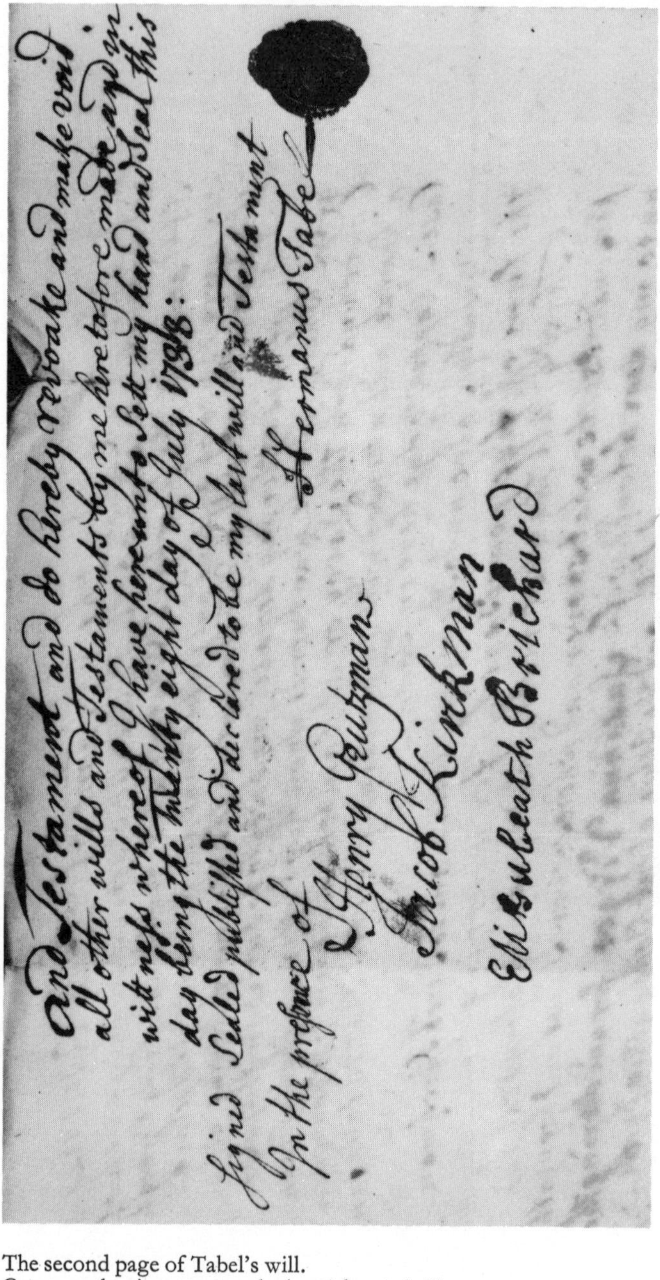

And Testament and do hereby revoake and make void all other wills and Testaments by one heretofore made and in wittness whereof I have hereunto sett my hand and seal this day being the twenty eight day of July 1758:

Hermanus Tabel

Signed Sealed published and declared to be my last will and Testament

In the presence of

Henry Bentzmans

Jacob Kirkman

Elisabeath Brickard

The second page of Tabel's will.
Compare the signature on the key (plate 49). Note also, the signature of Jacob Kirckman as one of the witnesses. *J. R. Freeman*

52

Tabel's seal from his will. Note the similarity to the
rose of the harpsichord (plate 50). *J. R. Freeman*

On Joes Karest's Virginal and the Origins of the Flemish Tradition

EDWIN M. RIPIN
Associate Professor of Music, Faculty of Arts and Science,
New York University

The origin of the Flemish harpsichord-building school, whose most characteristic products are the instruments made by the Ruckers family, presents simultaneously a baffling mystery and an irresistible challenge to anyone investigating the history of stringed keyboard instruments. Although the Ruckers name is inextricably associated with Flemish harpsichord-building, it is clear that none of the salient characteristics of the Flemish school can safely be credited to any member of the Ruckers family. Prototypes of the long-scaled, thick-cased Ruckers instruments were produced by the anonymous builder of the virginal made for the Duke of Cleves in 1568, by Hans Bos, by Hans Grawels, by Lodewijk Theeuwes, and presumably by Marten van der Biest and Hans Moermans the Elder as well, before Hans Ruckers entered the Guild of Saint Luke in 1579. The instruments being made by the other builders who petitioned the Guild for special recognition in 1557 may or may not have been similar, but there is good reason to suppose that some, at least, were not.

The only surviving pre-Ruckers instrument of the Flemish school, other than those cited, was made in 1548 by the builder whose name heads the 1557 petition. This instrument (plate 53), the polygonal virginal in the Musical Instrument Museum of the Royal Conservatory in Brussels inscribed IOES KAREST DE COLONIA,[1] is of the greatest interest in that it is so unlike the instruments one usually thinks of as Flemish. It has been dismissed as being 'much like an Italian spinet of the same period',[2] but this is less than completely accurate. The Karest virginal has an irregular hexagonal shape that does indeed remind one of Italian polygonal instruments, but it differs from Italian examples in having a completely inset keyboard.[3] The case is made of thin, brown wood and is finished at the top and bottom with elaborate mouldings rather heavier than those used on Italian instruments. The case is decorated inside and out with Latin mottoes—verses from Psalm 150—and the soundboard has two soundholes of different shapes underlayed by a pattern of crosses cut in parchment. The keyboard is covered with boxwood as on Italian instruments, but the keys are guided at the back by metal pins fitting into slots rather than by the wooden slips used by Italian makers. Unlike an Italian virginal, in which the jacks are guided by a single massive register, the jacks of the Karest virginal are guided at the top by leather-covered mortises in the soundboard and at the bottom by a second complete 'soundboard' mortised identically to the one on which the bridges rest. (This lower 'soundboard', set 63 mm (2½) below the visible one, apparently has no acoustical purpose whatever; it merely serves to guide the lower ends of the jacks.) Finally, the scaling of the Karest virginal is unlike that of mid-sixteenth-century Italian instruments. Karest's c″ string is 292 mm (11½) long, intermediate between the 254 mm (10) scale of most Italian harpsichords and the 356 mm (14) scale of standard Ruckers instruments.

Clearly, the Karest virginal has characteristics that constitute a curious mixture of those one generally associates with Italy and Flanders. However, since Karest's instrument predates those one thinks of as typically Flemish, this mixture of characteristics cannot be a historical blending. Rather, the later Flemish builders must have selected and emphasized certain characteristics of instruments like Karest's at the expense of others, making the scaling still longer and thickening the case, while retaining the inset keyboard and the guiding of the jacks by two thin registers.

This view presupposes that the Karest virginal, unique as it is among the surviving Flemish instruments, is truly representative of Flemish instrument-building in the middle of the sixteenth century. This point is established by four paintings dating from before 1565 (the only Flemish paintings known to this writer that show virginals in this period), all of which show instruments very like Karest's. Of these four paintings, the earliest and in many ways the most interesting is the portrait of a young girl playing a virginal (plate 54) painted by Catharina de Hemessen in 1548,[4] the same year in which the Karest instrument was built. The similarity of the instrument to Karest's is striking (despite its apparently smaller size), even extending to the presence of two differently shaped soundholes in the soundboard. Although the basic decor is different, the diagonally broken stripes on the jack rail are identical to those on the mouldings of the Karest.

Also noteworthy is the decorative use of a motto running around the inside of the case. The phrase shown, HABET ERGO MINUS, appears to be the end of the proverb 'Omnia dat dominus, non habet ergo minus',[5] which, together with SIC TRANSIT GLORIA MUNDI, also appears on a Flemish virginal signed A.W.H. that is preserved in the Accademia Santa Cecilia, Rome.[6] The proverb itself comes from the patristic literature, possible via the *Regimen moralitates*, a compendium that is known to have appeared in at least four printings before 1500.[7] The painted decor of arabesques alternating with pairs of stylized dolphins facing an urn strongly ties the instrument into the later tradition of Flemish harpsichord-building, since this design is the prototype of the 'sea-horse paper', familiar from many surviving Ruckers instruments and from such paintings as Vermeer's 'Music Lesson' in Buckingham Palace. (The earliest appearance of the paper itself is on a rectangular virginal made by Hans Bos in 1570, now in the Convento de Santa Clara at Tordesillas.) Although this pattern has yet to be traced to its exact source,[8] German and Flemish pattern books of the early sixteenth century reveal that its elements were among the most common Italian-inspired clichés of the period.[9]

The appearance of a design containing dolphins on musical instruments should not be surprising in view of the Classical association of dolphins with music, primarily in the identification of the dolphin with Apollo, but also because of the well-known legend of Arion's rescue from pirates by a dolphin drawn to the ship by Arion's song. This legend was sufficiently well known in the sixteenth century to inspire the title of Luis de Narváes' great collection of vihuela music, *Los seys libros del Delphín de música*, published at Valladolid in 1538, the title pages of which are adorned with a woodcut showing Arion riding the musical dolphin.[10]

The second Flemish painting to show a hexagonal virginal with an inset keyboard is the portrait of the van Berchem family (plate 55), which is attributed to Frans Floris and dated 1561.[11] Here, as in the Karest virginal and in the instrument in the de Hemessen portrait, the brown wood of the case serves as a background for the painted decoration. However, the doves, swags of flowers, and bundles of arrows, realistically reproduced in this decoration, represent an aesthetic different from that of the stylized dolphins shown in the de Hemessen portrait. The thin case and massive mouldings nonetheless emphasize its affinity with the Karest instrument. One especially important detail of this painting is the depiction of the strings of the virginal as grey lines, indicating that the instrument was strung with steel.

The third Flemish painting to show a hexagonal virginal is the large portrait, dated 1563, of Pierre Moucheron and his family (plate 56), attributed to Cornelis de Zeeuw.[12] The decoration of the instrument, part of which appears in the extreme foreground of the painting, is more like that shown in the de Hemessen portrait than that in the portrait of the van Berchem family. The outside of the case is decorated with arabesques, and the same motto appears to run round the inside of the case (with part of SIC TRANSIT GLORIA MUNDI on the jack rail).

The fourth Flemish painting that shows a hexagonal virginal is an unsigned family portrait (plate 57), painted in 1564, also attributed to de Zeeuw.[13] It shows an instrument decorated with painted dolphins like those in the de Hemessen portrait. The virginal differs in form from those shown in three earlier paintings in having one side that is in-curved (rather than having six straight sides) and in having ends that are perpendicular (rather than at acute angles) to the front.

The next Flemish representation of a virginal, an engraving by Cornelis Cort from a series devoted to the seven liberal arts,[14] depicts a rectangular instrument (plate 58), as do all subsequent representations known to this writer. However, the virginal shown in Cort's engraving has closer affinities with those just discussed than with the rectangular instruments shown in such later representations as Michiel Coxcie's 'St Cecilia' in the Prado Museum,[15] or the surviving Cleves and Bos virginals.[16] The case and soundboard of Cort's instrument are decorated in a manner similar to that shown in the portrait of the van Berchem family, and the instrument retains the massive bottom moulding seen in all the hexagonal examples, but lacking in both the surviving rectangular instruments and those shown in the later paintings. (This type of moulding seems to have fallen into disuse with the adoption of thick cases.) Furthermore, like virtually all thin-cased instruments, the virginal shown in the Cort engraving has no lid, whereas both the Cleves virginal and that shown in the Coxcie painting do. All in all, it seems reasonable to suppose that the thick-cased rectangular design replaced thin-cased hexagonal and rectangular types in the last years of the 1560s.

The search for instruments like the Karest virginal need not be confined solely to Flemish pictorial representations. A single Ruckers virginal[17] (significantly, an early one) is clearly based on the same design, although the long scaling, characteristic of Ruckers instruments, imparts a much slimmer and more graceful shape than is found in the earlier short-scaled instruments. However, an even more fruitful area of exploration exists if one looks outside Flanders, and in particular toward Germany. Van der Meer has analysed the surviving German sixteenth- and seventeenth-century instruments and representations, arriving at a highly significant group of characteristics that might be considered typically German.[18] These include thin cases with top and bottom mouldings, scaling intermediate to that of Italian and Ruckers instruments, decoration frequently consisting of painted designs for which the case wood provided the background, wood-topped natural keys, and (for virginals) inset keyboards. The parallel between these characteristics and those of the Karest and the similar virginals shown in the Flemish paintings is quite striking.

Two hexagonal virginals and a fascinating representation of a third have survived from Germany, and their similarity to Karest's would be difficult to exaggerate. Of the two surviving instruments, the one most clearly reminiscent of the Karest is a toy (plate 59) made *c.* 1639; [19] however, the full-sized instrument (plate 60) preserved in the Carolino Augusteum Museum in Salsburg [20] differs principally in having a lid, which probably explains the absence of any top moulding on the case. The German representation of a hexagonal virginal (plate 61) is the painting attributed to Friedrich von Falckenburg and dated 1619 [21] that decorated the lid of the outer case in which the instrument depicted was kept. Although the dimensions of the lid indicate that the instrument itself must have been a good deal larger than Karest's (probably owing to a C/E–f''' range rather than Karest's C/E–c'''), the German virginal is very much the same kind of instrument, despite the fact that it was built long after there is any reason to suppose such virginals were still being made in Flanders.

Even though these three German examples all date from the seventeenth century, it would seem rash to assume that they were modelled on mid-sixteenth-century Flemish virginals. Iconographic evidence indicates that the thin-cased instrument first came into being in Italy shortly before 1500. The intarsia representation of a clavichord in the *studiolo* of Federigo da Montefeltro executed between 1479 and 1482 shows a thick-cased instrument of the kind that appears to have been standard in the fifteenth century. The next Italian representations of a stringed keyboard instrument — an intarsia on a door to one of the Raphael *stanze* in the Vatican and the Giorgione or Titian 'Concert' in the Pitti Palace — date from about 1510 and show thin-cased instruments. Thus, the thin-cased design most probably emerged at some point in the thirty years preceding these two representations. Although the Flemish and German virginals differ from Italian instruments, they clearly take their inspiration from the Italian thin-cased model, and it is reasonable to assume that the instrument-building tradition they represent had its roots in Italy. Thus, one is left with the question of where this tradition acquired its non-Italian elements. Surprisingly, the available evidence on this question points to Germany rather than Flanders.

The earliest surviving stringed keyboard instrument built north of the Alps is German, not Flemish; moreover this instrument, inscribed GOTTES WORT BLEIBT EWICK BEISTEN DEN ARMEN ALS DEN REICHEN DURCH HANS MVLLER CV LEIPCIK IM 1537, [22] possesses many of the non-Italian characteristics of the Karest virginal, including jack-guiding by two thin registers. Considering the Müller harpsichord's early date, it is difficult to maintain the view that the Italian design came first to Flanders, where it acquired various non-Italian features, before being adopted in Germany. Furthermore, it should not be forgotten that Karest was a German who, fully twenty-one years after he had become a citizen of Antwerp in 1517, still signed himself 'de Colonia'. Germans were, of course, prominent in the instrument-building of the Low Countries in the sixteenth century. In fact, the German organ-builder Hans Süss, who came to Antwerp in 1509 to work on the new organ of the Church of Our Lady, has been identified as the Hans van Cuelen ('Hans from Cologne') who in 1512 made a 'clavicenon' for Eleanor of Austria, thus becoming Antwerp's first recorded harpsichord-builder.[23] The obvious inference to be drawn is that the Italian thin-cased design came first to Germany where it acquired a number of features that we generally think of as typically Flemish, and that it was then brought to Antwerp by Hans Süss or one of the other German instrument-builders working in Flanders in the early years of the sixteenth century.

If one seeks still farther afield for instruments similar to the Karest virginal, one finds that they are remarkably numerous. In fact, although no other hexagonal instruments with inset keyboards can be found, intermediate scaling, relatively thin cases, and the use of two thin jack guides are standard features of virtually all North European harpsichord-building before the ultimate triumph of long-scaled Ruckers-based designs toward the end of the seventeenth century. Despite the facts that particular instruments may vary widely from the norm and that such a standard design as the bentside spinet never lost its thick Italianate jack guide, the stylistic affinities among the instruments made in this widespread pre-Ruckers tradition heavily outweigh differences attributable to individual makers' tastes or national origins. Among the most prominent of these shared characteristics are the inset keyboard on transversely strung instruments, and the one-piece, round-tailed bentside and lute stop on harpsichords. The lute stop survives only in German and English instruments, but the round tail (although lacking in the Müller harpsichord) appears occasionally in France as well as in England. Like all the hexagonal virginals that have been the principal focus of this article, many of the instruments of this 'intermediate' tradition appear to have lacked lids and consequently must have been kept in outer cases. Iconographic evidence indicates that those rectangular instruments having lids generally had the vaulted type now familiar only from the late-seventeenth-century English virginals.

A full examination of the intermediate tradition is clearly beyond the scope of a short article, and the foregoing remarks are intended primarily to call attention to its existence and to suggest the central position of Germany in its development. The 1548 Karest virginal is one of the two earliest surviving products of this tradition—only the Müller harpsichord is older—and is its sole extant Flemish exemplar. Accordingly, its importance as a document in the history of the harpsichord is even greater than has heretofore been realized : in addition to being the oldest surviving Flemish virginal, it provides the sole tangible link between German and Flemish instrument-building in the first half of the sixteenth century.

NOTES AND REFERENCES

1   Catalogue no. 1587.
2   R. Russell *The Harpsichord and Clavichord* (London 1959) p. 42.
3   Some half-dozen sixteenth-century Italian polygonal virginals have their keyboards partly inset and thus bear a slight resemblance to the Karest virginal. All the other Italian polygonal virginals known to this writer have projecting keyboards.
4   In the Wallraf-Richartz Museum, Cologne : Catalogue no. 654.
5   I am indebted to Mr Howard Schott for suggesting this reconstruction of the proverb to me.
6   See D. H. Boalch *Makers of the Harpsichord and Clavichord* (London 1956) p. 39, and A. Cametti 'L'incipiente museo di strumenti musicali nella R. Accademia di S. Cecilia' *Annuario della Regia Accademia di Sta. Cecilia* v (1900) 27.
7   See H. Walter, ed., *Proverbia sententiaque latinitatis medii aevi* III (Gottingen 1963) p. 604, no. 19969, and W. A. Copinger *Supplement to Hain's Repertorium bibliographicum* (London 1895–1902) nos. 5040–5043. See also N. van der Blom 'De Latijnse teksten van De Scholier van Jan van Scorel' *Bulletin Museum Boymans* VIII (1957) 95–7, where it is suggested that the motto may have been taken from the writings of Erasmus and that the idea can be traced back to Plotinus.
8   See E. Closson 'L'Ornamentation en papier imprimé des clavecins anversois' *Revue belge d'archéologie et d'histoire de l'art* II (1932) 105–12, and D. F. L. Scheurleer 'Over het Ornament en de Authenticiteit van bedructe Papierstrooken en twee Clavierinstrumenten' *Medelingen van de Dienst voor Kunsten en Wetenschappen* VI, 45–9. Scheurleer traces several of the other designs from which the printed papers applied to instruments were made to *Variarum protactionum quas vulgo Marusias vocant libellus* of 1554, a pattern book by Balthasar Silvius of Antwerp.
9   See especially P. Jessen *Der Ornamentstich* (Berlin 1920), and R. Berliner *Ornamentale Vorlage-Blätter des 15. bis 18. Jahrhunderts* (Leipzig 1926). The use of the dolphin as a decorative motif on keyboard instruments was not restricted to the Low Countries. Emanuel Winternitz describes an Italian instrument of 1540 decorated with dolphins in 'A spinettina for the Duchess of Urbino' *Metropolitan Museum Journal* I (1968) 95–108.
10   However, see Adolfo Salazar 'Música, instrumentos, y danzas en las obras de Cervantes' *La Música en Cervantes y otros ensayos* (Madrid 196) p. 130n., where it is suggested that the title may be a reference to Prince Philip of Spain, called 'Delfín del Imperio' in the French manner. Narváes' title page is reproduced in *Die Musik in Geschichte und Gegenwart* I, cols. 623–4.

11   In the Museum Vuyts-van Campen and Baron Caroly, Lier. Regarding the attribution and date, L. van Puyvelde 'Floris ou Key? Le portrait de la famille van Berchem' *Musées royaux des beaux-arts de Belgique, Bulletin* (1965) pp. 197–204, has suggested that the painting is actually by Adrian Key, that the date (which appears as part of an inscription on the frame enclosing the painting rather than on the painting itself) may not be genuine, and that the picture may have been painted at any time between 1559 and 1568. Despite these objections, I am assured by Dr Carl van de Velde of Antwerp that there is no reason to doubt either the attribution to Floris or the genuineness of the date appearing on the frame.

12   In the Rijksmuseum, Amsterdam, Catalogue no. 2741–3–2. I am indebted to Dr P. J. J. van Thiel, Curator of the Paintings Department of the Rijksmuseum, for giving me access to this painting and for bringing to my attention the article by N. van der Blom cited in note 7.

13   In private ownership in Richmond, Surrey. I am indebted to Dr Jeannine Lambrechts-Douillez for bringing this painting to my attention.

14   The dating of this representation is difficult to establish. The engraving itself was published in 1565, but it is said to have been taken from a painting executed by Frans Floris some eleven years earlier. The Floris painting no longer exists, and one can only guess as to whether the instrument and its decoration were faithfully copied or were modernized when the engraving was made. See J. C. J. Bierens de Haan *L'œuvre gravé de Cornelis Cort, graveur hollandais, 1533–1578* (The Hague 1948) pp. 208–9.

15   Catalogue no. 1467. The painting is undated, but it is known to have been purchased by Philip II in 1569.

16   Photographs of the Cleves virginal are reproduced in R. Russell *Victoria and Albert Museum, Catalogue of Musical Instruments* I, *Keyboard Instruments* (London 1968) plate 11. A photograph of the Bos instrument is reproduced in *Carlos V y su ambiente : exposición en el iv centenario de su muerte* (Toledo 1958) plate CCLXXXIX.

17   Hans Ruckers, 1591 (Boalch no. 5). Photographs of this instrument are reproduced in Russell *The Harpsichord*, plate 24, and Boalch, op. cit., plate VIII.

18   J. H. van der Meer 'Beiträge zum Cembalobau im deutschen Sprachgebiet bis 1700' *Anzeiger des Germanischen Nationalmuseums* (1966) 103–33, esp. 126–7.

19   The instrument forms part of the furniture of a doll's-house in the Germanisches Nationalmuseum, Nürnberg.

20   See J. H. van der Meer 'Die Kielklaviere in Salzburger Museum Carolino Augusteum' *Salzburger Museum Carolino Augusteum, Jahresschrift* XII–XIII (1966–7) 87–8.

21   In the Germanisches Nationalmuseum, Nürnberg.

22   In the Raccolta Statali di Strumenti Musicali, Fondo Evan Gorga, Rome. The instrument is described in L. Cervelli and J. H. van der Meer *Conservato a Roma il piu antico clavicembalo tedesco* (Rome 1967).

23   See *Die Musik in Geschichte und Gegenwart* XII, cols. 1696–1697, and M. A. Vente *Die Brabanter Orgel* (Amsterdam 1958), where Hans' signature on the 1539 contract for the large organ of the Oude Kerk, Amsterdam, is reproduced on p. 69. The 1512 account entry concerning Eleanor's harpsichord was transcribed by E. van der Straeten *La Musique aux Pays-Bas avant le 19e siècle* VII

(Brussels 1885) p. 202, where Hans' name is erroneously given as 'van Ceulen'. The original document is now catalogued as B. 2224, fol. 408r, in the Archives Départementales du Nord, Lille.

53 Virginal by Joes Karest, 1548 (Musée Instrumental
de Bruxelles). *A.C.L., Brussels*

54

Catharina de Hemessen, 'Girl at a Spinet', 1548,
detail. *Wallraf-Richartz-Museum, Cologne*

Frans Floris, 'The van Berchem Family', 1581,
detail (Musea Wuyts-Van Campen en Baron
Caroly, Lier). *A.C.L., Brussels*

56

Cornelis de Zeeuw, 'Pierre Moucheron and his
Family', 1563, detail. *Rijksmuseum, Amsterdam*

57

Cornelis de Zeeuw, 'Family Portrait', 1564, detail.
Jack B. Gold, Richmond, Surrey

Cornelis Cort after Frans Floris, 'Musica', 1565,
detail. *Metropolitan Museum of Art, New York,
Harris Brisbane Dick Fund, 1928*

58

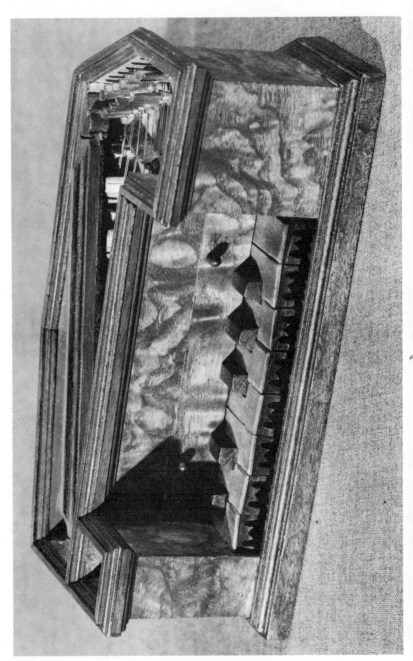

59

Anonymous toy virginal, *c.* 1639. *Germanisches Nationalmuseum, Nürnberg*

60
Anonymous German virginal.
Museum Carolino Augusteum, Salzburg

61

Friedrich van Falckenburg, 'Musical Society at
Nürnberg', 1619, detail. *Germanisches Nationalmuseum, Nürnberg*

The Earl of Wemyss' Claviorgan and its Context in Eighteenth-century England

PETER WILLIAMS
Director, The Russell Collection of Harpsichords and Clavichords, Edinburgh

Much information on the claviorgan, the composite organ-harpsichord, has appeared in recent years scattered through the standard sources, but no full study has emerged of an instrument which, though on the fringe of music-making, kept that place on the fringe for at least three centuries.[1] Before describing briefly what is undoubtedly the biggest, best-toned, and most important claviorgan still intact, the Kirckman-Snetzler made between 1745 and 1751 and belonging to the Earl of Wemyss (plate 62), it might be useful to sketch the eighteenth-century English background to this remarkable instrument. Paulirinus' *-nnportile* and the Spanish *claviórganos* of the fifteenth century, the Austrian clavichord-organs of the seventeenth century, and the French harmonium-pianos of the nineteenth century are the widest extremes of the claviorgan tradition; English instruments of the Georgian period were quite independent of those elsewhere and reflect nothing more cosmopolitan than the recurrent desire of keyboard-makers to invent and experiment.

The impression given by most English references of the period is that the instrument was not widely known. In one newspaper of 1733, there is mention of a 'curious Instrument lately invented' by an Oxford organist which could play, on one keyboard, 'two organs' and a harpsichord together or separately.[2] The stops were worked by foot-levers (though 'shifting movements' were still very rare in 1733), and together they provided thirty varieties of tone. Such a number smacks rather of theoretical computing (like Mersenne's organ registrations) than of practical timbre changes; but two organ stops and three sets of harpsichord strings would indeed give about thirty colours or combinations. Handel *may* have seen the organ while in Oxford that year, and it is certainly possible that his new organ concertos were written with an eye to performance on such instruments during the oratorio intervals. The keys of his chorus organ for *Saul* (1738) probably played a harpsichord for the recitatives and arias, although whether his instrument was a true claviorgan, or simply a box containing the trackers to the organ behind the choir, is uncertain.[3] Other composites of the period are known. Hipkins[4] wrote about that built in 1745 by Crang, which has been recently reconstructed;[5] however, although he claimed that 'there is no want of specimens', he cited only the Theeuwes in the Victoria and Albert Museum, the Crang and the harpsichord-organ used in the 1784 Handel Commemoration in Westminster Abbey. Similarly, his remark[6] that Shudi 'made such instruments occasionally in collaboration with the organ-builder Snetzler' has not been substantiated, although it is known that Snetzler and Shudi (both Swiss immigrants) were well acquainted and that Shudi worked on claviorgans.[7] This Shudi-Snetzler connection was first mentioned in Rees' *Cyclopaedia* (1819, under 'Shudi': 'Snetzler, who added horizontal organs to many of his harpsichords...'), probably by the chief music contributor, Charles Burney.

Typical of references to claviorgans is a letter of 1762 to the *Gentleman's Magazine* concerning 'an elegant desk' that

'Not only contains a little library of books...but an excellent fine-toned harpsichord, whose touch is remarkably good...we discovered behind the harpsichord a most compleat little organ, consisting of the stop *diapason* in wood, a *principal* and *fifteenth* in metal; these three stops, and the two unisons with the harpsichord, may be justly said to make an agreeable consort of itself, without the assistance of any other instrument. For the organ is not only made to swell but may be played together with the harpsichord, or each instrument separate, there being two setts of keys for that purpose, from *F in alt* down to *double Gamut*.'[8]

This instrument, built by the Bristol organ-builder John Kemys, was no doubt very expensive, for it was meant as a highly decorative piece of furniture with mirrors, bookcase, writing-desk attachment, and, on the musical side, some sort of swell mechanism. In Salisbury in 1765, a local builder, one Charles Green (probably unrelated to the illustrious Samuel Green) put an advertisement in the newspaper:

'To be sold by Charles Green, organ-builder and harpsichord-maker on the New Canal. A neat mahogany *Spinnet* with an *Organ*, so curiously contained in its Frame that it is scarce perceptible; and plays together, or separate with one set of Keys.'[9]

This was obviously a smaller instrument than the Bristol extravagance—perhaps an experiment, as was the recently reconstructed 1785 upright harpsichord made by R. Woffington of Dublin with one or more sets of organ pipes.[10]

Other theoretical sources suggest a certain amount of activity in this field. In the inventory of instruments confiscated during the Revolution in Paris, six of the sixty-four pianos (but none of the sixty-two harpsichords) were *organisé*.[11] Of those six, four were made in London; two by Berger (1788, 1775), one by Longman and Broderip, and one by Zumpe (1771)—all pianoforte-makers, not organ-builders.[12] The relative values imply that the English instruments were small. Almost ten per cent is a high proportion, however, and no doubt some people appreciated the value of an instrument suitable both for Sunday-evening psalm-singing and for mid-week consorts. Certainly Bédos had illustrated the claviorgan (both piano and harpsichord *organisé*) [13] as if it was a very common and practical instrument, and no doubt his pictures were well known in England together with the rest of the treatise. Burney had heard a claviorgan in use in a North Italian church but did not seem to find it very interesting. [14] Rees' *Cyclopaedia* contains no entries on the claviorgan, although it mentions other fringe instruments of less importance, such as the lyrichord and the claviol. [15] The later English dictionary-compilers sometimes included the organized pianoforte, as did Busby, Danneley, and Wilson, but with no details. Tans'ur in all his writings makes only one substantial reference, but it is one of particular interest in view of the occasional harpsichord-shaped chamber organ to be met with in late-eighteenth-century England — such as Samuel Green's for the Earl of Effingham (*c.* 1770) and that owned by the Marquis of Exeter (R. & W. Gray, 1790). [16] If the conversion of harpsichords to claviorgans was as simple as Tans'ur implies, the shape of those little instruments signifies that they may have been built for such conversion as occasion demanded:

'Some *Harpsichords* may be fixed over the Strikers [stickers] of the Palletts of an *Organ* to play both the *Organ* and the *Harpsichord* together with *one Set* of Keys; or either to be play'd alone, by moving the Keys forwards, or more back; a Hole being under to drop over the Sticker when the *Harpsichord* plays alone; which when pull'd out of the Hole forward, they both are play'd together, &c.' [17]

Tans'ur's just-intelligible remarks must not be taken to mean that this was a common practice, for suitable chamber organs were rare. Also interesting, however, in view of its rarity on English organs, is the mechanism described: the *Schiebekoppel*, the coupler that unites actions or keyboards by means of pushing or pulling one keyboard to fit over the other. Tans'ur may have known such an instrument, for I do not know any theoretical source from which he could have taken his description.

Many authors mention only the organized pianoforte type of claviorgan, but even this did not give complete satisfaction. R. J. S. Stevens tells in his diary of going to hear Michael Arne play an organ concerto (by his father?) in April 1784 at the Haymarket Little Theatre, during which he extemporized a fugue with

'sweepings of Chords, from the Bass to the upper part of the Instrument; which had a novel and an original effect. The Instrument he played upon was certainly against him; it appeared to me to be an Organized Piano Forte.' [18]

Whether or not such instruments were common in the theatres, they were certainly versatile and varied in effect. The largest clavi-organ of the time—if that is what it was—comprised the full harpsichord and large church organ used in Westminster Abbey at the Commemoration of Handel in 1784. Burney[19] said that the large organ at the back of the chorus and band had 'keys of communication with the harpsichord, at which Mr Bates, the conductor, was seated' at the front of the singers, near the soloists. These 'keys' were not actions to a separate soundboard but simply trackers underneath the harpsichord keys, probably connecting only with the Great Organ of Samuel Green's three-manual instrument. The terms of description resemble Burney's little account of Michele Todino's seventeenth-century organ-cum-harpsichord-cum-Geigenwerk-cum-spinet at Rome : a 'very fine harpsichord' which 'formerly had a communication with an organ in the same room, and with two spinets and a virginal'.[20]

A further example which demonstrates the hybrid's versatility was the instrument made by Hancock for John Marsh in 1781. This organ, a wealthy amateur's brain-child, had two consoles and several contrivances. There were two manuals, one for the organ and one for the pianoforte or 'piano-harp'

'so that I could make transitions from one to the other, or could to a *cantabile* treble on the swell of my organ play a kind of harp-accompaniment with my left hand on the piano-harp.'[21]

It is uncertain what this 'piano-harp' was, but little instruments of this name were mostly struck with hammers.[22] Whatever it was, it had a great fault:

'I soon however found an inconvenience I had not expected, viz. the difficulty of keeping pipes and strings in tune together, as the same alteration of weather, which would sharpen the one, would flatten the other. I therefore soon took it out, and let it stand upon a frame I had made for it, independent of the organ.'[23]

It might be thought that this was always the great imperfection of claviorgans : at St Michael's, Coventry, the organ of 1733 originally had a plucked-string stop (*harp, lute, and dulcimer* probably indicated a single set of strings) but had to have it removed thirty years later because of the 'difficulty of keeping the *strings* in tune'.[24]

This is, of course, the crippling disadvantage of claviorgans, which their putative musical application does not overcome. Irreconcilably odd though the combination of plucked strings and organ may sound to musicians—*pizzicato* movements of the figured-bass period were normally understood to be played *senza organo*—it is fair to point out that the biggest of such instruments were versatile in one specific way : they allowed many solo colours. Like the *Écho, Récit,* and *Cornet* manuals of seventeenth-century

French organs or the Swells of Spanish, English, and a few German organs, the claviorgan gave the player special effects for right-hand solos. For example, in the 'German flute' registration, the left hand plays harpsichord strings, the right hand a sustained or sprightly melody on the (usually) stopped wooden or metal pipes of the organ. Vice versa (harpsichord tune, organ accompaniment) was usually out of the question unless the right-hand tune was fast and highly figurative; the comparative strengths of the strings and pipes allow nothing less. Or the organ part could accompany pieces of a more solemn nature : such a claviorgan as that by H. W. Brock now in New York [25] (strings with one set of Gedackt pipes) was useful for, say, Handel's theatre oratorios, where the harpsichord was specified for recitatives and most arias, the organ for the choruses and certain characteristic arias. These instruments were no doubt played in many different ways, especially by the gentry who commissioned them; but it is surely wrong to over-state the usefulness of playing both parts of a claviorgan coupled together.

Some technical details of the Kirckman-Snetzler instrument follow, but its special tonal, historical, and musical qualities are not apparent from figures. It is an early work for both builders : 1744 is the earliest date of an extant Kirckman harpsichord, 1742 (doubtful) for a Snetzler organ in England. The precise relationship between *Tschudi, Schnetzler*, and *Kirchmann*; the particular reasons for the arrival in England between *c.*1718 and *c.*1740 of three instrument-makers from the same area of Europe (from Kirckman's Bischweiler in Lorraine-Germany through Snetzler's Schaffhausen to Shudi's Schwanden is only about 130 miles direct); their connection with other 'German' or near German makers such as the organ-builder Schreider, the piano-makers Backers and Zumpe, and the harpsichord-makers Tabel, Weber (Dublin), Shean (Schein?), and Neubauer—these are some of the biggest questions in eighteenth-century English instrument-making. The harpsichord and piano benefited from it; the organ did not, for Snetzler as a pupil of the Egedachers [26] had never really learnt what a well-voiced and well-planned organ was. His Tierce-Mixtures (an Austro-English compromise), his auxiliary chorus-stops, and his voicing of pipes at their feet did irreparable harm to the English organ—harm from which, indeed, it has never re-covered. A really good foreign builder such as Andreas Silber-mann, who worked in the Kirckman-Shudi area, [27] might have given a much-desired impetus to English native organ-building.

In 1748 Snetzler was still calling himself 'new to the trade' [28] and the organ part of the Wemyss claviorgan does not yet show the later characteristics of even the smallest Snetzler chamber (bureau) organs, such as Dulciana or divided Cornet/Sesquialtera stops. However, the open wood treble Diapason hints both at the English taste for solo melodic stops of the gentler kind and at the taste for 'auxiliary' stops, familiar in the areas of south-east Germany and the Danube, where Snetzler learnt his trade. The organ has two registration aids : a 'shifting movement' and a swell pedal. On his 1747/8 organ for the Moravians in Leeds, Snetzler also included these two devices, the Swell a complete little box containing four 8¹ solo stops more in the manner of south German *Echoes* (like that at Ochsenhausen, by J. Gabler, 1729–33) than of English Swells. The recorded payments for the Wemyss instrument (£86 6s.) must be for the organ and its transport and tuning only. Such a sumptuous harpsichord alone cost that sort of sum at this time, and Snetzler had no doubt progressed a little since 1747, when he charged 30 guineas for a tiny bureau organ for the Moravians in London (Fetter Lane Chapel).

The harpsichord has neither buff nor machine stops. Preliminary comparison with the 1744 harpsichord shows that the main areas of marquetry work (nameboard and the inside of the cheekpieces), the rose (intertwining J K, a monogram also incorporated in the nameboard marquetry), the chevron decoration of the lid and case, the position and style of the brass stop-knobs, the endblocks, and the inner decorative strips are remarkably similar in the two instruments. The similarity is so close that some parts might possibly be reverse inlays, the claviorgan having dark wood where the 1744 harpsichord has light wood and vice versa. However, the name batten and other surfaces are of a different marquetry pattern, and the question of reverse inlays cannot yet be answered. With a 1755 Kirckman,[29] we have a trio of similarly decorated instruments.

Although it is in playing order, the tone of the claviorgan is not at present entirely reliable historically, nor have I yet heard both instruments completely in tune together. The organ is soft, muffled, and underscaled; it seems to have been intended to supply either quiet solo colours or a gentle continuo for a small consort. It is probably fair to say that tonally the organ 'allows' for the harpsichord, whereas the harpsichord is an instrument in its own right.

Specification of the Kirckman-Snetzler Claviorgan

A finely inlaid claviorgan containing a two-manual harpsichord
(8, 8, 4, lute) and a reservoir-less chamber organ (8, 4, 2, 11 and
an 8 from c′) encased below the harpsichord, whose sides extend
to the ground.

Dimensions

Total length, 2527 mm (99½). The harpsichord projects at the
keyboard; the organ case projects at the tail. Length of harpsi-
chord ignoring mouldings, 2426 mm (95½).
Total width, 997 mm (39¼)
Width of harpsichord ignoring mouldings, 940 mm (37)
Total height including harpsichord lid, 1067 mm (42)
Height of organ case, 756 mm (29¾)

In the Wemyss Account Book

		£	s.	d.
16 November 1751				
paid John Snetzler Organ Builder in London		80	0	0
22 June 1754				
paid John Snetzler Organ Builder		6	6	0

Inscriptions

On nameboard: JACOBUS KIRCKMAN FECIT LONDINI
In the organ chest (at the back, Snetzler's usual place for
signature) : JOHAN SNETZLER FECIT LONDONI 1745

Eleven brass knobs at the keyboards
four above the upper manual (lute, 4′, dogleg 8′, lower 8′)
three to the left of the lower manual, let into the endblock
(open Diapason, stopped Diapason, Flute) two to the right
of the lower manual, let into the endblock (Fifteenth, Mixture)
two smaller knobs in front (l. and r.) of the lower manual,
together bringing into play the vertical stickers to the organ
pallets, connecting with a lug under each of the lower-manual
keys; pulling out connects the stickers.

Four foot-levers, three in front, one to the right side:
1. organ shifting movement shutting off the sliders of the two
metal stops.
2. bellows-lever.
3. swell-lever, pushing open the panel — 475 × 678 mm
(18 $\frac{11}{16}$ × 26 $\frac{11}{16}$) — below the right cheekpiece, and springing
back into position when the foot is removed.
4. auxiliary bellows-lever.

THE ORGAN, played from the lower manual (GG 10') [30]
Compass: GG to f''' (no GG♯)
Registers
 stopped wood Diapason 8'
 open wood Diapason 8' from c'
 stopped wood Flute 4'
 open metal Fifteenth 2'
 open metal Mixture II (19, 22; from c'' 12, 15)
Small foot-holes (since narrowed further), low cut-ups throughout, much shallow nicking.
Fifteenth, slightly larger scale than the treble 2' rank of the
Mixture; highly leaded pipes; bottom pipes mitred.
Chest size: 864 × 279 × 89 mm (34 × 11 × 3½)
The smaller pipes are placed upright to the player's front, on the
chest below the keyboards; the single-fold bellows are placed
below the chest, on the floor; the larger pipes are conducted off
by lead and wood conduits to lie horizontally below the harpsichord bottom; the open wood 8' pipes are placed vertically
behind the corner of the bentside.
Restored c. 1915, with several new pipes (copies?), especially
in the top open and stopped wood ranks.

THE HARPSICHORD
Compass: FF to f''' (no FF♯)
Registers (looking down on the instrument)
 ←4' lower
  8'→ lower
 ←8' dogleg
 ←8' lute, upper
Keyboards
Overall length of naturals:
 upper, 406 mm (16); 181 mm (7⅛) from front to balance pin.
 lower, 678 mm (26 11/16); 279 mm (11)
Length of natural playing surface:
 upper, 118 mm (4⅝)
 lower, 124 mm (4⅞)
Length of accidentals:
 upper, 73 mm (2⅞)
 lower, 81 mm (3 3/16)
Octave span: 164 mm (6 7/16)

Scaling[31]

Roughly conventional Kirckman from nut to bridge, but the case and soundboard are about 50 mm (2) longer than average— 200 mm (8) from bridge to tail—perhaps to allow access to the tuning tampions of the horizontal organ pipes below when the harpsichord is lifted off.

Note	Longer 8' string length		Plucking point (back 8')		Plucking point (lute)		4' string length		Plucking point	
	mm	inches	mm	inches	mm	inches	mm	inches	mm	inches
f'''	129	5 1/16	63	2 1/2	13	1/2	67	2 5/8	49	1 15/16
c'''	170	6 11/16	76	3	14	9/16	87	3 7/16	54	2 1/8
c''	337	13 1/4	92	3 5/8	17	11/16	175	6 7/8	67	2 5/8
c'	675	26 9/16	114	4 1/2	25	1	346	13 5/8	78	3 1/16
c	1156	45 1/2	133	5 1/4	38	1 1/2	597	23 1/2	92	3 5/8
C	1619	63 3/4	197	7 3/4	57	2 1/4	911	35 7/8	105	4 1/8
FF	1803	71	210	8 1/4	98	3 7/8	1044	41 1/8	111	4 3/8

String gauges

Written in ink on the nuts, several written more than once.

8' : 4 to c'', 5 c', 6 f, 7 c, 8 G, 9 E♭, 10 C, 11 BB♭, 12 GG♯, 13 FF.
4' : 4 to c'', 5 c', 6 e♭, 7 F♯, 8 BB, 9 AA, 10 GG, 11 FF.
Restored by W. R. Thomas in 1954.

NOTES AND REFERENCES

1   I am preparing a monograph on the claviorgan; meanwhile, much can be discovered in the works of Russell, Hubbard, van der Meer, van der Straeten, Sachs, Marcuse, Galpin, and others.
2   *Applebee's Original Weekly Journal*, 7 July 1733.
3   E.g. W. Dean *Handel's Dramatic Oratorios and Masques* (London 1959) pp. 110–11.
4   A. J. Hipkins *A Description and History of the Pianoforte and of Older Keyboard Stringed Instruments* (London-New York 1896) pp. 91 ff. See also R. Russell *The Harpsichord and Clavichord* (London 1959) p. 83.
5   In the collection of Dr Roger Mirrey, Redhill, Surrey.
6   Made also by E. F. Rimbault *The Pianoforte* (London 1860), p. 89.
7   Russell, op. cit., p. 83. Snetzler material will form part of a documentary history of the English organ now in preparation.
8   *The Gentleman's Magazine* XXXII (1762) 211.
9   *Salisbury Journal*, 2 April 1765.
10   M. Thomas 'The Claviorganum' *The Consort* XVI (1959) 29–32.

11 A. G. Hess 'The transition from harpsichord to piano' *Galpin Society Journal* VI (1953) 75.

12 Longman and Broderip, of course, hired out (and stuck their labels on) many barrel and finger organs, but there is no evidence of an organ workshop in the firm itself.

13 F. Bédos de Celles *L'Art du Facteur d'Orgues* IV (Paris 1778) plates CXXX–CXXXV.

14 P. A. Scholes *Dr Burney's Musical Tours in Europe* I (London 1959) p. 7.

15 A. Rees *The Cyclopaedia* (London 1819) under 'Instruments' and elsewhere.

16 Green's organ of 8, 4, 2, Dulciana (from c′) was restored by Noel Mander in 1958; the Grays' organ of 8, 4, 2, Sesquialtera, Cornet, Dulciana, Hautboy (the last three from c′, the Hautboy in a Swell box) is still in Burghley House.

17 W. Tans'ur *The Elements of Musick Display'd* (London 1772) under 'Harpsichord' in the dictionary section.

18 R. J. S. Stevens *Recollections* (MS in private possession) I, p. 119.

19 C. Burney *An account of the Musical Performances ... in Commemoration of Handel* (London 1785) p. 8.

20 Scholes, op. cit., pp. 301 ff. The instrument is illustrated by Todino, Bonanni (*Gabinetto Armonico* 1772), and others.

21 J. Marsh *Autobiography* (MS in private possession) IX–X, p. 850.

22 Hancock took out a patent in 1790 for an organized pianoforte (piano, flute and 'harp' stops — the latter probably a device coming into contact with the strings, *quasi arpicordo*); and in the *Musical Directory for the Year 1794*, he had himself listed as 'Organized Pia[noforte] Maker, Parliament St. Westminster'.

23 Marsh, op. cit.

24 E. J. Hopkins and E. F. Rimbault *The Organ* 3rd ed. (London 1877) p. 139

25 Such an instrument was actually suggested by Mattheson in the same area of Brock's northwest Germany. J. Mattheson *Der vollkommene Capellmeister* (Hamburg 1739) p. 484.

26 P. F. Williams *The European Organ 1450–1850* (London 1966) pp. 87–8, 276, 289.

27 Hubbard, op. cit., p. 175 seems to confuse the three chief Silbermanns — Andreas, Gottfried, and Johann Andreas.

28 W. L. Sumner 'John Snetzler and his first English Organs', *The Organ* XXXIII (1953–4) plate opposite p. 105, showing Snetzler's contract at the Fulneck Chapel, Leeds.

29 Russell, op. cit., plate 67. Now in the Russell Collection, Edinburgh.

30 Russell, op. cit., p. 83, gives the organ specification incorrectly.

31 Some figures were kindly supplied by Mr W. R. Thomas.

I would like to express my gratitude to the Earl of Wemyss and March, K.T., for allowing me to spend so much time with the instrument and to publish these details; also to Dr Roger Mirrey for information on both this claviorgan and his own Crang instrument.

The Earl of Wemyss' claviorgan (The Earl of
Wemyss). *Tom Scott*

A CATALOGUE OF
SELECTED DOVER BOOKS
IN ALL FIELDS OF INTEREST

A CATALOGUE OF SELECTED DOVER
BOOKS IN ALL FIELDS OF INTEREST

RACKHAM'S COLOR ILLUSTRATIONS FOR WAGNER'S RING. Rackham's finest mature work—all 64 full-color watercolors in a faithful and lush interpretation of the *Ring*. Full-sized plates on coated stock of the paintings used by opera companies for authentic staging of Wagner. Captions aid in following complete Ring cycle. Introduction. 64 illustrations plus vignettes. 72pp. 8⅝ x 11¼.   23779-6 Pa. $6.00

CONTEMPORARY POLISH POSTERS IN FULL COLOR, edited by Joseph Czestochowski. 46 full-color examples of brilliant school of Polish graphic design, selected from world's first museum (near Warsaw) dedicated to poster art. Posters on circuses, films, plays, concerts all show cosmopolitan influences, free imagination. Introduction. 48pp. 9⅜ x 12¼.
                                                        23780-X Pa. $6.00

GRAPHIC WORKS OF EDVARD MUNCH, Edvard Munch. 90 haunting, evocative prints by first major Expressionist artist and one of the greatest graphic artists of his time: *The Scream, Anxiety, Death Chamber, The Kiss, Madonna*, etc. Introduction by Alfred Werner. 90pp. 9 x 12.
                                                        23765-6 Pa. $5.00

THE GOLDEN AGE OF THE POSTER, Hayward and Blanche Cirker. 70 extraordinary posters in full colors, from Maitres de l'Affiche, Mucha, Lautrec, Bradley, Cheret, Beardsley, many others. Total of 78pp. 9⅜ x 12¼.   22753-7 Pa. $5.95

THE NOTEBOOKS OF LEONARDO DA VINCI, edited by J. P. Richter. Extracts from manuscripts reveal great genius; on painting, sculpture, anatomy, sciences, geography, etc. Both Italian and English. 186 ms. pages reproduced, plus 500 additional drawings, including studies for *Last Supper,* Sforza monument, etc. 860pp. 7⅞ x 10¾. (Available in U.S. only)
                              22572-0, 22573-9 Pa., Two-vol. set $15.90

THE CODEX NUTTALL, as first edited by Zelia Nuttall. Only inexpensive edition, in full color, of a pre-Columbian Mexican (Mixtec) book. 88 color plates show kings, gods, heroes, temples, sacrifices. New explanatory, historical introduction by Arthur G. Miller. 96pp. 11⅜ x 8½. (Available in U.S. only)   23168-2 Pa. $7.95

UNE SEMAINE DE BONTÉ, A SURREALISTIC NOVEL IN COLLAGE, Max Ernst. Masterpiece created out of 19th-century periodical illustrations, explores worlds of terror and surprise. Some consider this Ernst's greatest work. 208pp. 8⅛ x 11.   23252-2 Pa. $6.00

DRAWINGS OF WILLIAM BLAKE, William Blake. 92 plates from Book of Job, *Divine Comedy, Paradise Lost,* visionary heads, mythological figures, Laocoon, etc. Selection, introduction, commentary by Sir Geoffrey Keynes. 178pp. 8⅛ x 11. 22303-5 Pa. $4.00

ENGRAVINGS OF HOGARTH, William Hogarth. 101 of Hogarth's greatest works: *Rake's Progress, Harlot's Progress, Illustrations for Hudibras, Before and After, Beer Street and Gin Lane,* many more. Full commentary. 256pp. 11 x 13¾. 22479-1 Pa. $12.95

DAUMIER: 120 GREAT LITHOGRAPHS, Honore Daumier. Wide-ranging collection of lithographs by the greatest caricaturist of the 19th century. Concentrates on eternally popular series on lawyers, on married life, on liberated women, etc. Selection, introduction, and notes on plates by Charles F. Ramus. Total of 158pp. 9⅜ x 12¼. 23512-2 Pa. $6.00

DRAWINGS OF MUCHA, Alphonse Maria Mucha. Work reveals draftsman of highest caliber: studies for famous posters and paintings, renderings for book illustrations and ads, etc. 70 works, 9 in color; including 6 items not drawings. Introduction. List of illustrations. 72pp. 9⅜ x 12¼. (Available in U.S. only) 23672-2 Pa. $4.00

GIOVANNI BATTISTA PIRANESI: DRAWINGS IN THE PIERPONT MORGAN LIBRARY, Giovanni Battista Piranesi. For first time ever all of Morgan Library's collection, world's largest. 167 illustrations of rare Piranesi drawings—archeological, architectural, decorative and visionary. Essay, detailed list of drawings, chronology, captions. Edited by Felice Stampfle. 144pp. 9⅜ x 12¼. 23714-1 Pa. $7.50

NEW YORK ETCHINGS (1905-1949), John Sloan. All of important American artist's N.Y. life etchings. 67 works include some of his best art; also lively historical record—Greenwich Village, tenement scenes. Edited by Sloan's widow. Introduction and captions. 79pp. 8⅜ x 11¼. 23651-X Pa. $4.00

CHINESE PAINTING AND CALLIGRAPHY: A PICTORIAL SURVEY, Wan-go Weng. 69 fine examples from John M. Crawford's matchless private collection: landscapes, birds, flowers, human figures, etc., plus calligraphy. Every basic form included: hanging scrolls, handscrolls, album leaves, fans, etc. 109 illustrations. Introduction. Captions. 192pp. 8⅞ x 11¾. 23707-9 Pa. $7.95

DRAWINGS OF REMBRANDT, edited by Seymour Slive. Updated Lippmann, Hofstede de Groot edition, with definitive scholarly apparatus. All portraits, biblical sketches, landscapes, nudes, Oriental figures, classical studies, together with selection of work by followers. 550 illustrations. Total of 630pp. 9⅛ x 12¼. 21485-0, 21486-9 Pa., Two-vol. set $15.00

THE DISASTERS OF WAR, Francisco Goya. 83 etchings record horrors of Napoleonic wars in Spain and war in general. Reprint of 1st edition, plus 3 additional plates. Introduction by Philip Hofer. 97pp. 9⅜ x 8¼. 21872-4 Pa. $4.00

THE EARLY WORK OF AUBREY BEARDSLEY, Aubrey Beardsley. 157 plates, 2 in color: *Manon Lescaut, Madame Bovary, Morte Darthur, Salome,* other. Introduction by H. Marillier. 182pp. 8⅛ x 11. 21816-3 Pa. $4.50

THE LATER WORK OF AUBREY BEARDSLEY, Aubrey Beardsley. Exotic masterpieces of full maturity: *Venus and Tannhauser, Lysistrata, Rape of the Lock, Volpone,* Savoy material, etc. 174 plates, 2 in color. 186pp. 8⅛ x 11. 21817-1 Pa. $5.95

THOMAS NAST'S CHRISTMAS DRAWINGS, Thomas Nast. Almost all Christmas drawings by creator of image of Santa Claus as we know it, and one of America's foremost illustrators and political cartoonists. 66 illustrations. 3 illustrations in color on covers. 96pp. 8⅜ x 11¼. 23660-9 Pa. $3.50

THE DORÉ ILLUSTRATIONS FOR DANTE'S DIVINE COMEDY, Gustave Doré. All 135 plates from Inferno, Purgatory, Paradise; fantastic tortures, infernal landscapes, celestial wonders. Each plate with appropriate (translated) verses. 141pp. 9 x 12. 23231-X Pa. $4.50

DORÉ'S ILLUSTRATIONS FOR RABELAIS, Gustave Doré. 252 striking illustrations of *Gargantua and Pantagruel* books by foremost 19th-century illustrator. Including 60 plates, 192 delightful smaller illustrations. 153pp. 9 x 12. 23656-0 Pa. $5.00

LONDON: A PILGRIMAGE, Gustave Doré, Blanchard Jerrold. Squalor, riches, misery, beauty of mid-Victorian metropolis; 55 wonderful plates, 125 other illustrations, full social, cultural text by Jerrold. 191pp. of text. 9⅜ x 12¼. 22306-X Pa. $7.00

THE RIME OF THE ANCIENT MARINER, Gustave Doré, S. T. Coleridge. Dore's finest work, 34 plates capture moods, subtleties of poem. Full text. Introduction by Millicent Rose. 77pp. 9¼ x 12. 22305-1 Pa. $3.50

THE DORE BIBLE ILLUSTRATIONS, Gustave Doré. All wonderful, detailed plates: Adam and Eve, Flood, Babylon, Life of Jesus, etc. Brief King James text with each plate. Introduction by Millicent Rose. 241 plates. 241pp. 9 x 12. 23004-X Pa. $6.00

THE COMPLETE ENGRAVINGS, ETCHINGS AND DRYPOINTS OF ALBRECHT DURER. "Knight, Death and Devil"; "Melencolia," and more—all Dürer's known works in all three media, including 6 works formerly attributed to him. 120 plates. 235pp. 8⅜ x 11¼. 22851-7 Pa. $6.50

MECHANICK EXERCISES ON THE WHOLE ART OF PRINTING, Joseph Moxon. First complete book (1683-4) ever written about typography, a compendium of everything known about printing at the latter part of 17th century. Reprint of 2nd (1962) Oxford Univ. Press edition. 74 illustrations. Total of 550pp. 6⅛ x 9¼. 23617-X Pa. $7.95

THE COMPLETE WOODCUTS OF ALBRECHT DURER, edited by Dr. W. Kurth. 346 in all: "Old Testament," "St. Jerome," "Passion," "Life of Virgin," "Apocalypse," many others. Introduction by Campbell Dodgson. 285pp. 8½ x 12¼. 21097-9 Pa. $7.50

DRAWINGS OF ALBRECHT DURER, edited by Heinrich Wolfflin. 81 plates show development from youth to full style. Many favorites; many new. Introduction by Alfred Werner. 96pp. 8⅛ x 11. 22352-3 Pa. $5.00

THE HUMAN FIGURE, Albrecht Dürer. Experiments in various techniques—stereometric, progressive proportional, and others. Also life studies that rank among finest ever done. Complete reprinting of *Dresden Sketchbook*. 170 plates. 355pp. 8⅜ x 11¼. 21042-1 Pa. $7.95

OF THE JUST SHAPING OF LETTERS, Albrecht Dürer. Renaissance artist explains design of Roman majuscules by geometry, also Gothic lower and capitals. Grolier Club edition. 43pp. 7⅞ x 10¾ 21306-4 Pa. $3.00

TEN BOOKS ON ARCHITECTURE, Vitruvius. The most important book ever written on architecture. Early Roman aesthetics, technology, classical orders, site selection, all other aspects. Stands behind everything since. Morgan translation. 331pp. 5⅜ x 8½. 20645-9 Pa. $4.50

THE FOUR BOOKS OF ARCHITECTURE, Andrea Palladio. 16th-century classic responsible for Palladian movement and style. Covers classical architectural remains, Renaissance revivals, classical orders, etc. 1738 Ware English edition. Introduction by A. Placzek. 216 plates. 110pp. of text. 9½ x 12¾. 21308-0 Pa. $10.00

HORIZONS, Norman Bel Geddes. Great industrialist stage designer, "father of streamlining," on application of aesthetics to transportation, amusement, architecture, etc. 1932 prophetic account; function, theory, specific projects. 222 illustrations. 312pp. 7⅞ x 10¾. 23514-9 Pa. $6.95

FRANK LLOYD WRIGHT'S FALLINGWATER, Donald Hoffmann. Full, illustrated story of conception and building of Wright's masterwork at Bear Run, Pa. 100 photographs of site, construction, and details of completed structure. 112pp. 9¼ x 10. 23671-4 Pa. $5.50

THE ELEMENTS OF DRAWING, John Ruskin. Timeless classic by great Viltorian; starts with basic ideas, works through more difficult. Many practical exercises. 48 illustrations. Introduction by Lawrence Campbell. 228pp. 5⅜ x 8½. 22730-8 Pa. $3.75

GIST OF ART, John Sloan. Greatest modern American teacher, Art Students League, offers innumerable hints, instructions, guided comments to help you in painting. Not a formal course. 46 illustrations. Introduction by Helen Sloan. 200pp. 5⅜ x 8½. 23435-5 Pa. $4.00

THE ANATOMY OF THE HORSE, George Stubbs. Often considered the great masterpiece of animal anatomy. Full reproduction of 1766 edition, plus prospectus; original text and modernized text. 36 plates. Introduction by Eleanor Garvey. 121pp. 11 x 14¾. 23402-9 Pa. $6.00

BRIDGMAN'S LIFE DRAWING, George B. Bridgman. More than 500 illustrative drawings and text teach you to abstract the body into its major masses, use light and shade, proportion; as well as specific areas of anatomy, of which Bridgman is master. 192pp. 6½ x 9¼. (Available in U.S. only) 22710-3 Pa. $3.50

ART NOUVEAU DESIGNS IN COLOR, Alphonse Mucha, Maurice Verneuil, Georges Auriol. Full-color reproduction of *Combinaisons ornementales* (c. 1900) by Art Nouveau masters. Floral, animal, geometric, interlacings, swashes—borders, frames, spots—all incredibly beautiful. 60 plates, hundreds of designs. 9⅜ x 8-1/16. 22885-1 Pa. $4.00

FULL-COLOR FLORAL DESIGNS IN THE ART NOUVEAU STYLE, E. A. Seguy. 166 motifs, on 40 plates, from *Les fleurs et leurs applications decoratives* (1902): borders, circular designs, repeats, allovers, "spots." All in authentic Art Nouveau colors. 48pp. 9⅜ x 12¼. 23439-8 Pa. $5.00

A DIDEROT PICTORIAL ENCYCLOPEDIA OF TRADES AND INDUSTRY, edited by Charles C. Gillispie. 485 most interesting plates from the great French Encyclopedia of the 18th century show hundreds of working figures, artifacts, process, land and cityscapes; glassmaking, papermaking, metal extraction, construction, weaving, making furniture, clothing, wigs, dozens of other activities. Plates fully explained. 920pp. 9 x 12. 22284-5, 22285-3 Clothbd., Two-vol. set $40.00

HANDBOOK OF EARLY ADVERTISING ART, Clarence P. Hornung. Largest collection of copyright-free early and antique advertising art ever compiled. Over 6,000 illustrations, from Franklin's time to the 1890's for special effects, novelty. Valuable source, almost inexhaustible.
Pictorial Volume. Agriculture, the zodiac, animals, autos, birds, Christmas, fire engines, flowers, trees, musical instruments, ships, games and sports, much more. Arranged by subject matter and use. 237 plates. 288pp. 9 x 12. 20122-8 Clothbd. $14..50

Typographical Volume. Roman and Gothic faces ranging from 10 point to 300 point, "Barnum," German and Old English faces, script, logotypes, scrolls and flourishes, 1115 ornamental initials, 67 complete alphabets, more. 310 plates. 320pp. 9 x 12. 20123-6 Clothbd. $15.00

CALLIGRAPHY (CALLIGRAPHIA LATINA), J. G. Schwandner. High point of 18th-century ornamental calligraphy. Very ornate initials, scrolls, borders, cherubs, birds, lettered examples. 172pp. 9 x 13. 20475-8 Pa. $7.00

ART FORMS IN NATURE, Ernst Haeckel. Multitude of strangely beautiful natural forms: Radiolaria, Foraminifera, jellyfishes, fungi, turtles, bats, etc. All 100 plates of the 19th-century evolutionist's *Kunstformen der Natur* (1904). 100pp. 9⅜ x 12¼.   22987-4 Pa. $5.00

CHILDREN: A PICTORIAL ARCHIVE FROM NINETEENTH-CENTURY SOURCES, edited by Carol Belanger Grafton. 242 rare, copyright-free wood engravings for artists and designers. Widest such selection available. All illustrations in line. 119pp. 8⅜ x 11¼.
23694-3 Pa. $4.00

WOMEN: A PICTORIAL ARCHIVE FROM NINETEENTH-CENTURY SOURCES, edited by Jim Harter. 391 copyright-free wood engravings for artists and designers selected from rare periodicals. Most extensive such collection available. All illustrations in line. 128pp. 9 x 12.
23703-6 Pa. $4.50

ARABIC ART IN COLOR, Prisse d'Avennes. From the greatest ornamentalists of all time—50 plates in color, rarely seen outside the Near East, rich in suggestion and stimulus. Includes 4 plates on covers. 46pp. 9⅜ x 12¼.   23658-7 Pa. $6.00

AUTHENTIC ALGERIAN CARPET DESIGNS AND MOTIFS, edited by June Beveridge. Algerian carpets are world famous. Dozens of geometrical motifs are charted on grids, color-coded, for weavers, needleworkers, craftsmen, designers. 53 illustrations plus 4 in color. 48pp. 8¼ x 11. (Available in U.S. only)   23650-1 Pa. $1.75

DICTIONARY OF AMERICAN PORTRAITS, edited by Hayward and Blanche Cirker. 4000 important Americans, earliest times to 1905, mostly in clear line. Politicians, writers, soldiers, scientists, inventors, industrialists, Indians, Blacks, women, outlaws, etc. Identificatory information. 756pp. 9¼ x 12¾.   21823-6 Clothbd. $40.00

HOW THE OTHER HALF LIVES, Jacob A. Riis. Journalistic record of filth, degradation, upward drive in New York immigrant slums, shops, around 1900. New edition includes 100 original Riis photos, monuments of early photography. 233pp. 10 x 7⅞.   22012-5 Pa. $7.00

NEW YORK IN THE THIRTIES, Berenice Abbott. Noted photographer's fascinating study of city shows new buildings that have become famous and old sights that have disappeared forever. Insightful commentary. 97 photographs. 97pp. 11⅜ x 10.   22967-X Pa. $5.00

MEN AT WORK, Lewis W. Hine. Famous photographic studies of construction workers, railroad men, factory workers and coal miners. New supplement of 18 photos on Empire State building construction. New introduction by Jonathan L. Doherty. Total of 69 photos. 63pp. 8 x 10¾.
23475-4 Pa. $3.00

THE DEPRESSION YEARS AS PHOTOGRAPHED BY ARTHUR ROTH-
STEIN, Arthur Rothstein. First collection devoted entirely to the work of
outstanding 1930s photographer: famous dust storm photo, ragged children,
unemployed, etc. 120 photographs. Captions. 119pp. 9¼ x 10¾.
23590-4 Pa. $5.00

CAMERA WORK: A PICTORIAL GUIDE, Alfred Stieglitz. All 559 illustrations and plates from the most important periodical in the history of
art photography, Camera Work (1903-17). Presented four to a page, reduced in size but still clear, in strict chronological order, with complete
captions. Three indexes. Glossary. Bibliography. 176pp. 8⅜ x 11¼.
23591-2 Pa. $6.95

ALVIN LANGDON COBURN, PHOTOGRAPHER, Alvin L. Coburn. Revealing autobiography by one of greatest photographers of 20th century
gives insider's version of Photo-Secession, plus comments on his own work.
77 photographs by Coburn. Edited by Helmut and Alison Gernsheim.
160pp. 8⅛ x 11.
23685-4 Pa. $6.00

NEW YORK IN THE FORTIES, Andreas Feininger. 162 brilliant photographs by the well-known photographer, formerly with Life magazine, show
commuters, shoppers, Times Square at night, Harlem nightclub, Lower
East Side, etc. Introduction and full captions by John von Hartz. 181pp.
9¼ x 10¾.
23585-8 Pa. $6.95

GREAT NEWS PHOTOS AND THE STORIES BEHIND THEM, John
Faber. Dramatic volume of 140 great news photos, 1855 through 1976,
and revealing stories behind them, with both historical and technical information. Hindenburg disaster, shooting of Oswald, nomination of Jimmy
Carter, etc. 160pp. 8¼ x 11.
23667-6 Pa. $5.00

THE ART OF THE CINEMATOGRAPHER, Leonard Maltin. Survey of
American cinematography history and anecdotal interviews with 5 masters—
Arthur Miller, Hal Mohr, Hal Rosson, Lucien Ballard, and Conrad Hall.
Very large selection of behind-the-scenes production photos. 105 photographs. Filmographies. Index. Originally Behind the Camera. 144pp.
8¼ x 11.
23686-2 Pa. $5.00

DESIGNS FOR THE THREE-CORNERED HAT (LE TRICORNE),
Pablo Picasso. 32 fabulously rare drawings—including 31 color illustrations
of costumes and accessories—for 1919 production of famous ballet. Edited
by Parmenia Migel, who has written new introduction. 48pp. 9⅜ x 12¼.
(Available in U.S. only)
23709-5 Pa. $5.00

NOTES OF A FILM DIRECTOR, Sergei Eisenstein. Greatest Russian
filmmaker explains montage, making of Alexander Nevsky, aesthetics; comments on self, associates, great rivals (Chaplin), similar material. 78 illustrations. 240pp. 5⅜ x 8½.
22392-2 Pa. $4.50

HOLLYWOOD GLAMOUR PORTRAITS, edited by John Kobal. 145 photos capture the stars from 1926-49, the high point in portrait photography. Gable, Harlow, Bogart, Bacall, Hedy Lamarr, Marlene Dietrich, Robert Montgomery, Marlon Brando, Veronica Lake; 94 stars in all. Full background on photographers, technical aspects, much more. Total of 160pp. 8⅜ x 11¼. 23352-9 Pa. $6.00

THE NEW YORK STAGE: FAMOUS· PRODUCTIONS IN PHOTO-GRAPHS, edited by Stanley Appelbaum. 148 photographs from Museum of City of New York show 142 plays, 1883-1939. *Peter Pan, The Front Page, Dead End, Our Town*, O'Neill, hundreds of actors and actresses, etc. Full indexes. 154pp. 9½ x 10. 23241-7 Pa. $6.00

DIALOGUES CONCERNING TWO NEW SCIENCES, Galileo Galilei. Encompassing 30 years of experiment and thought, these dialogues deal with geometric demonstrations of fracture of solid bodies, cohesion, leverage, speed of light and sound, pendulums, falling bodies, accelerated motion, etc. 300pp. 5⅜ x 8½. 60099-8 Pa. $4.00

THE GREAT OPERA STARS IN HISTORIC PHOTOGRAPHS, edited by James Camner. 343 portraits from the 1850s to the 1940s: Tamburini, Mario, Caliapin, Jeritza, Melchior, Melba, Patti, Pinza, Schipa, Caruso, Farrar, Steber, Gobbi, and many more—270 performers in all. Index. 199pp. 8⅜ x 11¼. 23575-0 Pa. $7.50

J. S. BACH, Albert Schweitzer. Great full-length study of Bach, life, background to music, music, by foremost modern scholar. Ernest Newman translation. 650 musical examples. Total of 928pp. 5⅜ x 8½. (Available in U.S. only) 21631-4, 21632-2 Pa., Two-vol. set $11.00

COMPLETE PIANO SONATAS, Ludwig van Beethoven. All sonatas in the fine Schenker edition, with fingering, analytical material. One of best modern editions. Total of 615pp. 9 x 12. (Available in U.S. only) 23134-8, 23135-6 Pa., Two-vol. set $15.50

KEYBOARD MUSIC, J. S. Bach. Bach-Gesellschaft edition. For harpsichord, piano, other keyboard instruments. English Suites, French Suites, Six Partitas, Goldberg Variations, Two-Part Inventions, Three-Part Sinfonias. 312pp. 8⅛ x 11. (Available in U.S. only) 22360-4 Pa. $6.95

FOUR SYMPHONIES IN FULL SCORE, Franz Schubert. Schubert's four most popular symphonies: No. 4 in C Minor ("Tragic"); No. 5 in B-flat Major; No. 8 in B Minor ("Unfinished"); No. 9 in C Major ("Great"). Breitkopf & Hartel edition. Study score. 261pp. 9⅜ x 12¼. 23681-1 Pa. $6.50

THE AUTHENTIC GILBERT & SULLIVAN SONGBOOK, W. S. Gilbert, A. S. Sullivan. Largest selection available; 92 songs, uncut, original keys, in piano rendering approved by Sullivan. Favorites and lesser-known fine numbers. Edited with plot synopses by James Spero. 3 illustrations. 399pp. 9 x 12. 23482-7 Pa. $9.95

PRINCIPLES OF ORCHESTRATION, Nikolay Rimsky-Korsakov. Great classical orchestrator provides fundamentals of tonal resonance, progression of parts, voice and orchestra, tutti effects, much else in major document. 330pp. of musical excerpts. 489pp. 6½ x 9¼.   21266-1 Pa. $7.50

TRISTAN UND ISOLDE, Richard Wagner. Full orchestral score with complete instrumentation. Do not confuse with piano reduction. Commentary by Felix Mottl, great Wagnerian conductor and scholar. Study score. 655pp. 8⅛ x 11.   22915-7 Pa. $13.95

REQUIEM IN FULL SCORE, Giuseppe Verdi. Immensely popular with choral groups and music lovers. Republication of edition published by C. F. Peters, Leipzig, n. d. German frontmaker in English translation. Glossary. Text in Latin. Study score. 204pp. 9⅜ x 12¼.
23682-X Pa. $6.00

COMPLETE CHAMBER MUSIC FOR STRINGS, Felix Mendelssohn. All of Mendelssohn's chamber music: Octet, 2 Quintets, 6 Quartets, and Four Pieces for String Quartet. (Nothing with piano is included). Complete works edition (1874-7). Study score. 283 pp. 9⅜ x 12¼.
23679-X Pa. $7.50

POPULAR SONGS OF NINETEENTH-CENTURY AMERICA, edited by Richard Jackson. 64 most important songs: "Old Oaken Bucket," "Arkansas Traveler," "Yellow Rose of Texas," etc. Authentic original sheet music, full introduction and commentaries. 290pp. 9 x 12.   23270-0 Pa. $7.95

COLLECTED PIANO WORKS, Scott Joplin. Edited by Vera Brodsky Lawrence. Practically all of Joplin's piano works—rags, two-steps, marches, waltzes, etc., 51 works in all. Extensive introduction by Rudi Blesh. Total of 345pp. 9 x 12.   23106-2 Pa. $14.95

BASIC PRINCIPLES OF CLASSICAL BALLET, Agrippina Vaganova. Great Russian theoretician, teacher explains methods for teaching classical ballet; incorporates best from French, Italian, Russian schools. 118 illustrations. 175pp. 5⅜ x 8½.   22036-2 Pa. $2.50

CHINESE CHARACTERS, L. Wieger. Rich analysis of 2300 characters according to traditional systems into primitives. Historical-semantic analysis to phonetics (Classical Mandarin) and radicals. 820pp. 6⅛ x 9¼.
21321-8 Pa. $10.00

EGYPTIAN LANGUAGE: EASY LESSONS IN EGYPTIAN HIERO-GLYPHICS, E. A. Wallis Budge. Foremost Egyptologist offers Egyptian grammar, explanation of hieroglyphics, many reading texts, dictionary of symbols. 246pp. 5 x 7½. (Available in U.S. only)
21394-3 Clothbd. $7.50

AN ETYMOLOGICAL DICTIONARY OF MODERN ENGLISH, Ernest Weekley. Richest, fullest work, by foremost British lexicographer. Detailed word histories. Inexhaustible. Do not confuse this with Concise Etymological Dictionary, which is abridged. Total of 856pp. 6½ x 9¼.
21873-2, 21874-0 Pa., Two-vol. set $12.00

A MAYA GRAMMAR, Alfred M. Tozzer. Practical, useful English-language grammar by the Harvard anthropologist who was one of the three greatest American scholars in the area of Maya culture. Phonetics, grammatical processes, syntax, more. 301pp. 5⅜ x 8½.   23465-7 Pa. $4.00

THE JOURNAL OF HENRY D. THOREAU, edited by Bradford Torrey, F. H. Allen. Complete reprinting of 14 volumes, 1837-61, over two million words; the sourcebooks for *Walden*, etc. Definitive. All original sketches, plus 75 photographs. Introduction by Walter Harding. Total of 1804pp. 8½ x 12¼.   20312-3, 20313-1 Clothbd., Two-vol. set $70.00

CLASSIC GHOST STORIES, Charles Dickens and others. 18 wonderful stories you've wanted to reread: "The Monkey's Paw," "The House and the Brain," "The Upper Berth," "The Signalman," "Dracula's Guest," "The Tapestried Chamber," etc. Dickens, Scott, Mary Shelley, Stoker, etc. 330pp. 5⅜ x 8½.   20735-8 Pa. $4.50

SEVEN SCIENCE FICTION NOVELS, H. G. Wells. Full novels. *First Men in the Moon, Island of Dr. Moreau, War of the Worlds, Food of the Gods, Invisible Man, Time Machine, In the Days of the Comet.* A basic science-fiction library. 1015pp. 5⅜ x 8½. (Available in U.S. only)
                                    20264-X Clothbd. $8.95

ARMADALE, Wilkie Collins. Third great mystery novel by the author of *The Woman in White* and *The Moonstone*. Ingeniously plotted narrative shows an exceptional command of character, incident and mood. Original magazine version with 40 illustrations. 597pp. 5⅜ x 8½.
                                    23429-0 Pa. $6.00

MASTERS OF MYSTERY, H. Douglas Thomson. The first book in English (1931) devoted to history and aesthetics of detective story. Poe, Doyle, LeFanu, Dickens, many others, up to 1930. New introduction and notes by E. F. Bleiler. 288pp. 5⅜ x 8½. (Available in U.S. only)
                                    23606-4 Pa. $4.00

FLATLAND, E. A. Abbott. Science-fiction classic explores life of 2-D being in 3-D world. Read also as introduction to thought about hyperspace. Introduction by Banesh Hoffmann. 16 illustrations. 103pp. 5⅜ x 8½.
                                    20001-9 Pa. $2.00

THREE SUPERNATURAL NOVELS OF THE VICTORIAN PERIOD, edited, with an introduction, by E. F. Bleiler. Reprinted complete and unabridged, three great classics of the supernatural: *The Haunted Hotel* by Wilkie Collins, *The Haunted House at Latchford* by Mrs. J. H. Riddell, and *The Lost Stradivarious* by J. Meade Falkner. 325pp. 5⅜ x 8½.
                                    22571-2 Pa. $4.00

AYESHA: THE RETURN OF "SHE," H. Rider Haggard. Virtuoso sequel featuring the great mythic creation, Ayesha, in an adventure that is fully as good as the first book, *She*. Original magazine version, with 47 original illustrations by Maurice Greiffenhagen. 189pp. 6½ x 9¼.
                                    23649-8 Pa. $3.50

UNCLE SILAS, J. Sheridan LeFanu. Victorian Gothic mystery novel, considered by many best of period, even better than Collins or Dickens. Wonderful psychological terror. Introduction by Frederick Shroyer. 436pp. 5⅜ x 8½.   21715-9 Pa. $6.00

JURGEN, James Branch Cabell. The great erotic fantasy of the 1920's that delighted thousands, shocked thousands more. Full final text, Lane edition with 13 plates by Frank Pape. 346pp. 5⅜ x 8½.
23507-6 Pa. $4.50

THE CLAVERINGS, Anthony Trollope. Major novel, chronicling aspects of British Victorian society, personalities. Reprint of Cornhill serialization, 16 plates by M. Edwards; first reprint of full text. Introduction by Norman Donaldson. 412pp. 5⅜ x 8½.   23464-9 Pa. $5.00

KEPT IN THE DARK, Anthony Trollope. Unusual short novel about Victorian morality and abnormal psychology by the great English author. Probably the first American publication. Frontispiece by Sir John Millais. 92pp. 6½ x 9¼.   23609-9 Pa. $2.50

RALPH THE HEIR, Anthony Trollope. Forgotten tale of illegitimacy, inheritance. Master novel of Trollope's later years. Victorian country estates, clubs, Parliament, fox hunting, world of fully realized characters. Reprint of 1871 edition. 12 illustrations by F. A. Faser. 434pp. of text. 5⅜ x 8½.   23642-0 Pa. $5.00

YEKL and THE IMPORTED BRIDEGROOM AND OTHER STORIES OF THE NEW YORK GHETTO, Abraham Cahan. Film *Hester Street* based on *Yekl* (1896). Novel, other stories among first about Jewish immigrants of N.Y.'s East Side. Highly praised by W. D. Howells—Cahan "a new star of realism." New introduction by Bernard G. Richards. 240pp. 5⅜ x 8½.   22427-9 Pa. $3.50

THE HIGH PLACE, James Branch Cabell. Great fantasy writer's enchanting comedy of disenchantment set in 18th-century France. Considered by some critics to be even better than his famous *Jurgen*. 10 illustrations and numerous vignettes by noted fantasy artist Frank C. Pape. 320pp. 5⅜ x 8½.   23670-6 Pa. $4.00

ALICE'S ADVENTURES UNDER GROUND, Lewis Carroll. Facsimile of ms. Carroll gave Alice Liddell in 1864. Different in many ways from final Alice. Handlettered, illustrated by Carroll. Introduction by Martin Gardner. 128pp. 5⅜ x 8½.   21482-6 Pa. $2.50

FAVORITE ANDREW LANG FAIRY TALE BOOKS IN MANY COLORS, Andrew Lang. The four Lang favorites in a boxed set—the complete *Red, Green, Yellow* and *Blue* Fairy Books. 164 stories; 439 illustrations by Lancelot Speed, Henry Ford and G. P. Jacomb Hood. Total of about 1500pp. 5⅜ x 8½.   23407-X Boxed set, Pa. $15.95

HOUSEHOLD STORIES BY THE BROTHERS GRIMM. All the great Grimm stories: "Rumpelstiltskin," "Snow White," "Hansel and Gretel," etc., with 114 illustrations by Walter Crane. 269pp. 5⅜ x 8½.

21080-4 Pa. $3.50

SLEEPING BEAUTY, illustrated by Arthur Rackham. Perhaps the fullest, most delightful version ever, told by C. S. Evans. Rackham's best work. 49 illustrations. 110pp. 7⅞ x 10¾. 22756-1 Pa. $2.50

AMERICAN FAIRY TALES, L. Frank Baum. Young cowboy lassoes Father Time; dummy in Mr. Floman's department store window comes to life; and 10 other fairy tales. 41 illustrations by N. P. Hall, Harry Kennedy, Ike Morgan, and Ralph Gardner. 209pp. 5⅜ x 8½. 23643-9 Pa. $3.00

THE WONDERFUL WIZARD OF OZ, L. Frank Baum. Facsimile in full color of America's finest children's classic. Introduction by Martin Gardner. 143 illustrations by W. W. Denslow. 267pp. 5⅜ x 8½.

20691-2 Pa. $3.50

THE TALE OF PETER RABBIT, Beatrix Potter. The inimitable Peter's terrifying adventure in Mr. McGregor's garden, with all 27 wonderful, full-color Potter illustrations. 55pp. 4¼ x 5½. (Available in U.S. only)

22827-4 Pa. $1.25

THE STORY OF KING ARTHUR AND HIS KNIGHTS, Howard Pyle. Finest children's version of life of King Arthur. 48 illustrations by Pyle. 131pp. 6⅛ x 9¼. 21445-1 Pa. $4.95

CARUSO'S CARICATURES, Enrico Caruso. Great tenor's remarkable caricatures of self, fellow musicians, composers, others. Toscanini, Puccini, Farrar, etc. Impish, cutting, insightful. 473 illustrations. Preface by M. Sisca. 217pp. 8⅜ x 11¼. 23528-9 Pa. $6.95

PERSONAL NARRATIVE OF A PILGRIMAGE TO ALMADINAH AND MECCAH, Richard Burton. Great travel classic by remarkably colorful personality. Burton, disguised as a Moroccan, visited sacred shrines of Islam, narrowly escaping death. Wonderful observations of Islamic life, customs, personalities. 47 illustrations. Total of 959pp. 5⅜ x 8½.

21217-3, 21218-1 Pa., Two-vol. set $12.00

INCIDENTS OF TRAVEL IN YUCATAN, John L. Stephens. Classic (1843) exploration of jungles of Yucatan, looking for evidences of Maya civilization. Travel adventures, Mexican and Indian culture, etc. Total of 669pp. 5⅜ x 8½. 20926-1, 20927-X Pa., Two-vol. set $7.90

AMERICAN LITERARY AUTOGRAPHS FROM WASHINGTON IRVING TO HENRY JAMES, Herbert Cahoon, et al. Letters, poems, manuscripts of Hawthorne, Thoreau, Twain, Alcott, Whitman, 67 other prominent American authors. Reproductions, full transcripts and commentary. Plus checklist of all American Literary Autographs in The Pierpont Morgan Library. Printed on exceptionally high-quality paper. 136 illustrations. 212pp. 9⅛ x 12¼. 23548-3 Pa. $12.50

CATALOGUE OF DOVER BOOKS

AN AUTOBIOGRAPHY, Margaret Sanger. Exciting personal account of
hard-fought battle for woman's right to birth control, against prejudice,
church, law. Foremost feminist document. 504pp. 5⅜ x 8½.
20470-7 Pa. $5.50

MY BONDAGE AND MY FREEDOM, Frederick Douglass. Born as a
slave, Douglass became outspoken force in antislavery movement. The
best of Douglass's autobiographies. Graphic description of slave life. Introduction by P. Foner. 464pp. 5⅜ x 8½. 22457-0 Pa. $5.50

LIVING MY LIFE, Emma Goldman. Candid, no holds barred account by
foremost American anarchist: her own life, anarchist movement, famous
contemporaries, ideas and their impact. Struggles and confrontations in
America, plus deportation to U.S.S.R. Shocking inside account of perse-
cution of anarchists under Lenin. 13 plates. Total of 944pp. 5⅜ x 8½.
22543-7, 22544-5 Pa., Two-vol. set $12.00

LETTERS AND NOTES ON THE MANNERS, CUSTOMS AND CON-
DITIONS OF THE NORTH AMERICAN INDIANS, George Catlin. Classic
account of life among Plains Indians: ceremonies, hunt, warfare, etc.
Dover edition reproduces for first time all original paintings. 312 plates.
572pp. of text. 6⅛ x 9¼. 22118-0, 22119-9 Pa.. Two-vol. set $12.00

THE MAYA AND THEIR NEIGHBORS, edited by Clarence L. Hay,
others. Synoptic view of Maya civilization in broadest sense, together with
Northern, Southern neighbors. Integrates much background, valuable detail not elsewhere. Prepared by greatest scholars: Kroeber, Morley, Thompson, Spinden, Vaillant, many others. Sometimes called Tozzer Memorial
Volume. 60 illustrations, linguistic map. 634pp. 5⅜ x 8½.
23510-6 Pa. $10.00

HANDBOOK OF THE INDIANS OF CALIFORNIA, A. L. Kroeber.
Foremost American anthropologist offers complete ethnographic study of
each group. Monumental classic. 459 illustrations, maps. 995pp. 5⅜ x 8½.
23368-5 Pa. $13.00

SHAKTI AND SHAKTA, Arthur Avalon. First book to give clear, co-
hesive analysis of Shakta doctrine, Shakta ritual and Kundalini Shakti
(yoga). Important work by one of world's foremost students of Shaktic
and Tantric thought. 732pp. 5⅜ x 8½. (Available in U.S. only)
23645-5 Pa. $7.95

AN INTRODUCTION TO THE STUDY OF THE MAYA HIEROGLYPHS,
Syvanus Griswold Morley. Classic study by one of the truly great figures
in hieroglyph research. Still the best introduction for the student for reading Maya hieroglyphs. New introduction by J. Eric S. Thompson. 117 illustrations. 284pp. 5⅜ x 8½. 23108-9 Pa. $4.00

A STUDY OF MAYA ART, Herbert J. Spinden. Landmark classic inter-
prets Maya symbolism, estimates styles, covers ceramics, architecture,
murals, stone carvings as artforms. Still a basic book in area. New introduction by J. Eric Thompson. Over 750 illustrations. 341pp. 8⅜ x 11¼.
21235-1 Pa. $6.95

GEOMETRY, RELATIVITY AND THE FOURTH DIMENSION, Rudolf Rucker. Exposition of fourth dimension, means of visualization, concepts of relativity as Flatland characters continue adventures. Popular, easily followed yet accurate, profound. 141 illustrations. 133pp. 5⅜ x 8½.
23400-2 Pa. $2.75

THE ORIGIN OF LIFE, A. I. Oparin. Modern classic in biochemistry, the first rigorous examination of possible evolution of life from nitrocarbon compounds. Non-technical, easily followed. Total of 295pp. 5⅜ x 8½.
60213-3 Pa. $4.00

PLANETS, STARS AND GALAXIES, A. E. Fanning. Comprehensive introductory survey: the sun, solar system, stars, galaxies, universe, cosmology; quasars, radio stars, etc. 24pp. of photographs. 189pp. 5⅜ x 8½. (Available in U.S. only)
21680-2 Pa. $3.75

THE THIRTEEN BOOKS OF EUCLID'S ELEMENTS, translated with introduction and commentary by Sir Thomas L. Heath. Definitive edition. Textual and linguistic notes, mathematical analysis, 2500 years of critical commentary. Do not confuse with abridged school editions. Total of 1414pp. 5⅜ x 8½.
60088-2, 60089-0, 60090-4 Pa., Three-vol. set $18.50

Prices subject to change without notice.

Available at your book dealer or write for free catalogue to Dept. GI, Dover Publications, Inc., 180 Varick St., N.Y., N.Y. 10014. Dover publishes more than 175 books each year on science, elementary and advanced mathematics, biology, music, art, literary history, social sciences and other areas.